Holy
TRANSFORMATION

Holy TRANSFORMATION

What it takes for
God to make a
difference
in *you*

CHIP INGRAM

MOODY PUBLISHERS
CHICAGO

Library of Congress Cataloging-in-Publication Data

Ingram, Chip, 1954-
    Holy transformation : what it takes for God to make a difference in you / by Chip Ingram.
        p. cm.
    Includes bibliographical references.
    ISBN 0-8024-2979-3
    1. Christian life. I. Title.

BV4501.3 .I54 2003
248.4--dc21

                                        2002151842

1 3 5 7 9 10 8 6 4 2

Printed in the United States of America

I dedicate this book to my sister Punkie,
whose new life in Christ was such a picture of
Holy Transformation
that I was drawn to the source of her "changed life,"
Jesus.
Thank you, sis!

CONTENTS

ACKNOWLEDGMENTS

I'd like to thank Dawson Troutman, Cameron Townsend, Hudson Taylor, Francis Schaeffer, Charles R. Soloman, Lewis Sperry Chafer, Howard Hendricks, John Ortberg, and Dallas Willard for instructing me in the truth of *Holy Transformation.*

I'd like to thank my wife, Theresa, my children, my friends, the staff of Santa Cruz Bible Church, the staff of *Living on the Edge,* and my mentors for helping me learn to appropriate the truth of Holy Transformation in everyday life.

And finally, I'd like to thank writer/editor Neil Wilson, my assistant Annette Kypreos, and Greg Thornton and the Moody team for making the truth of Holy Transformation available to others.

INTRODUCTION

The fact that you picked up this book tells me we have something in common—we both care about change. You wouldn't pick up a book titled *Holy Transformation* if changing and growing were not important to you.

This book is not simply about change, though. It is not a self-help book. These pages were not written to help you lose a few pounds or gain some additional motivation for your next project. These chapters will not describe how you can simply become more fulfilled or successful. This book is about holy transformation. If you want to know what it takes for God to make a difference in you, you have come to the right place. This book is about the very core of the Christian life. It is about the promise Jesus made that we could have life and have it more abundantly.

The Scripture states emphatically, "Therefore, if anyone is in Christ, he is a new creation; old things have passed away; behold, all things have become new" (2 Corinthians 5:17 NKJV). Unfortunately, this concept isn't working very well in American Christianity. All the best research by Barna and Gallup tells us that those who claim to know Jesus Christ as their personal savior in America are not changing very much at all. Their character seems untouched by their conversion: their marriages continue to deteriorate, their families fail, their personal lives display chaos and self-destructive behaviors such as pornography, workaholism, infidelity, and a lack of spiritual vitality. Christians themselves are struggling with the question: "How can we claim that Christ makes a difference in our lives when our lives don't really look much different from the rest of society?" Until we can answer that question clearly, we will continue to cast doubt on the validity of the very gospel we proclaim.

So what's wrong? What does it take for God to make a difference in us? Why is the average Christian so anemic when it comes to authentic, supernatural, spiritual transformation? If those questions interest you, I invite you to join me on a journey where we will discover together what holy transformation is and how it actually works.

The promises in Scripture about definitive transformation are clear. When a person is in Christ, there are predictable and supernatural changes from the inside out that we not only hope for but *expect* to happen in each of our lives. Yes, it is a process. Yes, it does take time. And no, it's not easy. But Christ's presence does bring about changes that are beyond anything cosmetic in nature. These changes are the kind that only God can bring about! Your participation is important, but the end result of holy transformation in your heart, mind, and life will represent God's gracious work in you. As you experience holy transformation, you will know it isn't you. Others will remark about the changes they see. The more you keep track of what God actually does in you, the more you will be absolutely astounded when you look back in several years. You will remember who you were—but you will definitely not be the same kind of person any more. That's the startling effect of holy transformation!

Before we go on, please understand this. I'm not talking about becoming more religious or exerting more willpower to read your Bible more often or pray for longer periods of time. I'm also not talking about wishing you could sing, speak, or perform athletic feats like well-known celebrities. I'm not even talking about good and healthy changes in eating or exercise habits that might be beneficial to you and your family. Those changes, wonderful as they are, can often be achieved through positive thinking, a strong will, and a good dose of self-discipline.

The kind of change I'm talking about involves the supernatural. Our goal is not a "remodeled" you accomplished through hard work and self-effort, but a "brand new you" that thinks, acts, and feels differently because the Spirit of God has taken up residence within you. What I'm talking about is the kind of change that you can't fake and is so radical that you are the first to know that it is Christ in you that's making the difference.

Allow me to paint a few word pictures to describe the kind of change we're talking about.

PICTURE #1

Imagine coming home after an absolutely exhausting and stressful day. You close the door to the world and lean against it for a moment. Relief. It's time to unwind. A flashing light on the answering machine catches your attention. You press the button as you kick off your shoes.

Before you even recognize the voice, you feel the tension in it. It belongs to a not-so-close friend with a desperate SOS. Tom needs help, and he called you.

Funny thing, though. You immediately experience a shift of focus off yourself and your difficult day. You are filled with a rather sudden compassion for old Tom. Energy seems to flow from nowhere. You find yourself that evening helping someone in a way that changes a life. You arrive back at home outwardly exhausted, but inwardly refreshed. There's no human explanation for the depth of your love and compassion for the person you just helped. You are nearly as amazed by your response as Tom was. In a matter of a few hours you experienced as well as gave supernatural, unconditional love. Can you imagine that?

PICTURE #2

You hear the good news of an astonishing windfall only to realize that the recipient of this good fortune is someone who has done you wrong in the past. There's no mistake. Someone who hurt you deeply has just cashed in on life's lottery.

Now picture this: the immediate, powerful reaction that comes to your mind is one of joy and gratitude for God's blessing on this person. It's not a realization that you *should* respond that way. You really *are* happy for them. In the aftermath of that reaction, an overwhelming sense of peace envelops your soul, confirming that the long road of forgiving them has finally come to an end.

A close friend observes your reaction, questions your sanity, and wants to know how you can possibly be happy for someone who has treated you so badly. Can you imagine that?

PICTURE #3

This one will take more imagination. As the result of an unexpected development—your death—you suddenly find yourself able to hear the honest conversations of your children and closest friends as they gather at your home after your funeral. They describe you as one of the most patient, faithful, Christlike people they have ever known. These aren't the common platitudes or exaggerations that people tend to say after funerals. The heartfelt comments reveal that you actually became the kind of person that we all long to become—loving and strong. They describe your joy, accepting attitude, and fun-loving outlook. They express tearful appreciation for your integrity, faithfulness to God, and loyalty to people. They talk about your heart, your warmth, and your passion for both the lovely and the unlovely of this world. Can you imagine realizing that your life was so changed, so transformed, that you were a little mirror of Christ while on this planet? Your life was so dominated by God's Spirit that you authentically reflected His presence. Can you imagine that?

CAN IMAGINATION BECOME REALITY?

Do you realize that this kind of supernatural transformation is not the stuff of saints and superstars, but available to every person in whom His Spirit dwells? It is my hope that these mental images awaken a deep longing in you. I hope you say, "Yeah, I'd like that to be true of me." It's possible, you know. God's Word outlines a game plan so that what I just described can actually happen in your life. It's about Christ actually being formed in you. It's achievable. In fact, it's so possible that it represents God's will for every person.

What I just described you can't fake. It goes way beyond behavior modification. Did you notice what was missing in those "Can You Imagines?" There was no mention of cleaning up your morality, or curbing your cussing, or even changing a few inward attitudes. Nobody talked about giving a little money to charity, going to church more often, or setting records for prayer and Bible reading. That's because what I'm describing is not something that someone, even someone committed to a cause, can do through mere discipline. I'm talking about something that's supernatural—inside-out change. You can't invent godly compassion. You can't fake an attitude of gratitude that comes to your mind when someone who has deeply wounded you is blessed. Those responses mean something has happened in your heart.

People who sit around after a funeral in private, honest conversations and speak highly about a person from the heart bear witness to God's work in someone's life. There's nothing to lose, there's no one to impress. God says He wants to change you. He wants to change you into the person you long to become. He's got a game plan to bring about the best in His children. Throughout this book we will look at God's design for morphing His people into the character of Jesus Christ.

WHY IS CHANGE NOT OCCURRING?

Why aren't the lives of Christians changing like the pictures I just described? Why do the stories above illustrate what we long to be and what the Scriptures clearly teach, and yet not what we actually experience in daily life?

Again, here are the sobering statistics: Barna, Gallup, and others are reporting that the kind of radical life transformation that we are describing in this book only occurs in the lives of about 10 percent of American Christians. Many long for it; few are experiencing it.

Something is wrong. Something is terribly wrong —but it doesn't have to stay that way. You long to change, and God wants you to change! He doesn't want you to simply clean up the outside of the cup, learn some Christian lingo, and be a better moral person. He wants to transform your heart and your desires, give you love and power, and form the very character of Jesus within you. This is a book about you experiencing that in your life. This is about holy transformation. This is about what it takes for God to make a difference in you. These pages will take you on a journey to help you discover the "whats" and the "hows" of holy transformation in a normal, ordinary Christian's life like yours and mine.

A PROMISE

I'm not offering you "pie in the sky" in this book. I'm not asking you to be open to something abnormal, never-been-tried spiritual secret. This is not a hidden mystery given only to a few gurus, or some new spiritual plan that has you trying harder than ever before only to be disappointed again.

You will learn what the apostle Paul taught the Ephesian church in the first century. This book is based solely on the God-inspired teaching that moved an ordinary group of have-nots, slaves, and persecuted people to be so radically transformed that they "turned their world upside down." They lived with such winsome love and holy boldness that people recognized them as "having been with Jesus."

This material has been "test driven" by those in the local church in which I have taught for the last twelve years and by many who listen to our nationwide radio ministry *Living on the Edge*. When the biblical truths in this book are applied, remarkable change *happens* in people's lives. On my desk as I write this sits a stack of e-mails and letters that describe the holy transformation God continues to carry out in people's lives all over America and beyond, who have put the content of this book into practice. I've included some of their stories. They come from every imaginable background, social strata, and economic status. Wherever you are right now, God has holy transformation in mind for you. He's in the business of spiritual metamorphosis!

I have come to realize that the average Christian simply does not know how spiritual growth and transformation really occurs. Somewhere along the line, the clear teaching of Ephesians 4 has been replaced by hopeless busyness. Well-meaning people go to church, try hard to be good, read their Bibles, pray as best they can, but secretly live in quiet desperation over the reminders that, though they deeply long to change, their lives remain much the same.

Well, if you are serious about change (and I mean *real* change), and if you long for supernatural change that occurs by God's Spirit making the old things pass away and (watch this!) **all things becoming new** (see 2 Corinthians 5:17), then let's begin this journey together.

1
WHAT DOES A
CHANGED LIFE LOOK LIKE?

In order for you to understand how holy transformation occurs, you need a completely different picture of how God works in your life. God has included an object lesson in nature that gives the exact word He uses when He describes a transformed life. God's Word says, "Do not conform any longer to the pattern of this world, but be *transformed* by the renewing of your mind" (Romans 12:2, emphasis added). That passage tells us that breaking the world's pattern or mold and allowing ourselves to be transformed will not only include a renewed mind but will also "test and approve what God's will is—his good, pleasing and perfect will." In other words, *transformation* means we will become what God wants us to become!

The word translated "transformed" in the verse above is the Greek word *metamorphoō*. God's Word actually instructs us to be morphed, or changed.

This word and the amazing natural process it describes help us to begin to think quite differently and more accurately about how God brings about spiritual change in our lives. This single word provides the key for understanding how spiritual transformation occurs. It directly challenges our ideas about trying harder to live holy lives. It emphasizes God's power and participation in our transformation. Our way leads to frustration, failure, and disappointment. God's way leads to metamorphosis: a changed life. Which one do you want to experience?

ROLL THE TAPE!

A time-lapse photographer captured with exquisite care the process through which a caterpillar becomes a butterfly. I showed the tape to several large groups to visually introduce what I call the process of spiritual morphing. We shared a wonder unfolding before our eyes. In less than two minutes we watched a sequence of change and struggle that actually lasted several days. Some miracles happen so slowly that we don't notice them until we see them in high speed. Let me describe it for you.

The opening shot brings us face to mandible with an awkward, pondering, many-humped worm. The worm rapidly devours the leaf on which it is sitting. Then it seems to stop for a break, hanging tentatively from a stem. The next action begins at the caterpillar's other end. A silk strand appears, and the caterpillar begins gyrating, wrapping itself in the fine thread. Soon the worm has disappeared into its self-made enclosure, suspended in air. The light behind the pouch shifts and we note that the contents seem transparent. The caterpillar turns out to be a magician. He's gone.

But wait! The pouch suddenly appears to blush, then darken. It's moving. The cocoon splits, unable to contain its struggling contents. A creature emerges, at first even less attractive than the caterpillar—dark, wet, quivering. As if in agony, the tiny living thing unfolds. Collapsed umbrella-like, a wing magically takes shape and stiffens. A matching one follows. Dazzling patterns and colors appear. Fragile legs begin to move as the gossamer marvel shifts to the top-side of the stem. The wings flex, testing the air currents. Suddenly, gone! The plant still vibrates slightly from the butterfly's liftoff. Another camera, taping in real time, captures our ex-caterpillar flitting between flowers, exulting in its freedom, dancing on the wind. The transformation speaks such joy that we can't decide whether to cheer for the creature, cry over the beauty, envy the freedom, or bow in gratitude to the Creator.

The time-lapse video allows us to see one of the greatest miracles in nature. Something starts out as an ugly worm and turns into a beautiful butterfly. A creature that crawls ends up as a creature that flies. A living creature takes on a new nature. The caterpillar doesn't go anywhere in order to change completely. The worm dies, or so it appears, in order for the butterfly to emerge. In the hidden transformation chamber of the cocoon, a green, crawling creature clinging to a branch becomes a beautiful, multicolored butterfly that soars beneath the sun.

What would it be like to go through such drastic change? God's Word tells us that we can find out. This miracle of creation parallels God's work in our lives. In fact, the very same word used to describe this transformation in nature is also used by the Holy Spirit to describe God's intention and command for every one of His spiritual children. That word is *metamorphosis,* or *morphing,* for short. God has it in mind for you.

WHAT IS MORPHING?

A metallic liquid pool rises from the floor to take the shape of a man. One distinct animal flows into the form of another. A recognizable face seems to melt seamlessly into another familiar face. We see these transformations happen in advertisements, films, and even news reports every day. When images are recorded as digital bits of information, they can be manipulated into any shape. Filmmakers who discovered this amazing technique decided to call it *morphing.* They didn't invent the word—they borrowed it.

Morph comes from the Greek language. As a noun (*morphē*), the word refers to the unique form or nature of something or someone. In the New Testament, it is used to describe Jesus. "Who, being in *very nature* God, did not consider equality with God something to be grasped, but made himself nothing, taking the *very nature* of a servant, being made in human likeness" (Philippians 2:6–7, emphasis added). The verb (*morphoō*) doesn't refer to the external shape but rather to the inward form or essence of a person. This inward essence is not readily changed without extraordinary or divine work. "My dear children, for whom I am again in the pains of childbirth until Christ is *formed* in you" (Galatians 4:19, emphasis added), Paul writes to his friends. He was praying and hoping for their morphing. He was praying for what God wants to do in every life—including yours.

WHY DO WE ALL LONG TO MORPH?

Jesus said, "I have come that they may have life, and that they may have it more abundantly" (John 10:10 NKJV). The transformation implied by the difference between "having life" and "having it more abundantly" requires morphing. The caterpillar and the butterfly share the same life, but the butterfly has reached the "more abundant" experience of life.

Morphing describes God's goal for the Christian's life: to transform you into the image of Jesus. The Scriptures describe the beginning of that process with various words. The moment you came to Christ, you were saved and forgiven, and the Spirit of God entered your heart. God's game plan from that point on uses every circumstance, every person, every disappointment, every bit of suffering, and every touch of joy to conform (morph) you into the very likeness of His Son (see Romans 8:29; Ephesians 2:10).

Even those people who don't yet know Christ long to be morphed. The clues in our culture are obvious. Self-help books and seminars have grown into a multibillion-dollar industry because we're made in the image of our Creator and long to recapture what is now missing. Something inside each of us says, "I want to change. I want to grow. I want to do better. I want to be better!" I've never met anyone who says, "You know, I'm not a very good parent, and I'd like to get worse." People don't say, "I'm an average golfer, but I'd like to raise my handicap." Couples don't look into each other's eyes and say, "You know, honey, we have a good marriage, but maybe we could communicate less and work toward a divorce in five years." No, the desire for positive change is relentless.

SPIRITUAL METAMORPHOSIS

Every person wants to grow and develop, even if they don't use those terms to describe the desire. The reason isn't hard to find. The spiritual DNA in our souls is God-given. We were designed to change. What we often lack is direction and encouragement. These also come from God. Philippians 2:13 says, "For it is God who is at work in you, both to will and to work for His good pleasure" (NASB).

Similar to what we see in nature, spiritual metamorphosis usually involves three major stages:

- **First, there is birth**—the initial stage (John 3:1–16; 2 Corinthians 5:17). Spiritually, that's when Jesus becomes your Savior. Your sins are forgiven, you are justified in God's sight, the Holy Spirit takes up residence within you, and you become part of the family of God. You are spiritually born!

- **Second,** after birth there is a process that leads to **spiritual maturity** (Philippians 1:6; Colossians 2:6–7). In this stage you begin to significantly reflect the person and character of Christ. The fruit of the Spirit's work within you progressively yields love, joy, peace, and patience in your heart as well as in your relationships with others.

- **Third,** as you continue to grow, you will become more a part of the **disciple-making process.** This is called spiritual reproduction (Matthew 28:19–20; 2 Timothy 2:2). Like everything in the animal kingdom, a sign of real maturity is the capacity to reproduce. At that point, Jesus is not only your Lord, but He also uses you in the process of birthing and growing other new believers.

UNDERSTANDING MORPHING

The worm-to-butterfly process gives us an illustration of spiritual metamorphosis, but the entire process has to be understood at a personal level. It is not enough to explain it in theological jargon or in such glowing experiential language that we honestly wonder if it's possible at all.

So, allow me to give you a realistic picture of spiritual metamorphosis through the life of a friend that I have known for over ten years. Consider this story of my friend Geoff to be a time-lapse review of God's morphing work in one person's life. As I describe Geoff's spiritual birth, growth to maturity, and spiritual reproduction, ask yourself, *Where am I in God's spiritual morphing process?*

GEOFF'S STORY

Geoff is a good friend with an unusual spelling for the name Jeff. If you met Geoff today, you would observe a man entering middle age with stability, calm, and a contented smile on his face most of the time. You wouldn't know, unless you asked, the chaos in his background. You wouldn't appreciate, unless you listened, the remarkable transformation that brought him out of a destructive childhood, a downward-spiraling early adulthood, and a life of wreckage to where he lives today. But Geoff would be the first to tell you that nothing in his life today is a credit to his persistence, wisdom, efforts, or abilities. He knows that God has transformed his life.

Geoff grew up in a broken home. An absent father and an alcoholic mother provided little sense of parental care. His mother attempted suicide several times during his childhood. In unconscious ways he imitated his mother's self-destructive behaviors. He remembers his years from high school into his thirties as a haze of alcohol, drugs, and strange experiences with cults. Broken relationships littered these decades of his life.

Geoff's early success with his own business was poisoned by his tendency to make rash and unwise decisions. Both his business and his body suffered increasing difficulties because of his choices. He had to declare bankruptcy. His kidneys began to fail, overwhelmed by the flow of chemicals he was ingesting. Geoff showed all the signs of a lost and wasted life.

At some point during the final downhill slide, Geoff met Will South, a man who expressed an unexpected and genuine interest in a down-and-out. Will stepped in to care for Geoff at a time when Geoff didn't care too much for himself. Surrounded by the garbage and consequences of his past, Geoff noticed that Will was remarkably different from the people and the problems he was used to dealing with. The first time Geoff heard Will pray for him—out loud, by name—something began to awaken in his heart. Life had never been darker for Geoff, but Will's presence seemed like a distant light that offered a way out.

Will eventually introduced Geoff to other Christians with solid qualities and character in their lives. Geoff felt loved and accepted, but he also became more keenly aware of the vacuum in his own life. He could see flaws in their lives, but he knew there was something happening in them that wasn't happening in him. They had hope; he felt hopeless. They seemed to have direction; he had none. He couldn't bring himself to put out the effort to be good; they didn't seem to have to put out an effort to accept and welcome him. Out of that awareness, Geoff realized he desperately needed what these Christians had. And when he asked, he discovered they were happy and eager to explain that he could simply acknowledge

his need to God and receive complete forgiveness
and eternal life through a personal relationship with
Jesus Christ.

Geoff's surrender to Christ created an almost immediate sense of security, meaning, and purpose in
his life. Most of his troubles were still around him,
but he experienced genuine joy and peace for the
first time in his life.

Unfortunately, the spiritual birth that Geoff experienced at his lowest point is sometimes viewed
as the end instead of the beginning of spiritual life.
Just like a baby is born into the world to grow up and
fulfill his destiny, so all of us when we are spiritually
born are really beginning a long process of spiritual
metamorphosis, not arriving at the end. The tragedy
is that many people have understood that they are
sinners before God and that Christ has paid the
penalty for their sin. They have repented and turned
to Christ for the forgiveness of their sin, asked Him
to come into their lives, and been spiritually born.
Yet they have been led to believe that what they have
just experienced is the extent of the Christian life.
Their condition actually resembles that of a newborn
whose mother leaves him on the delivery table without love, milk, or constant care, saying instead, "I
had the birth. Isn't that it?"

Just as birth is the beginning of physical life,
spiritual birth is the exciting beginning of a whole
new way of living that leads to maturity and Christlikeness. Birth starts the process. That's what Geoff
discovered once he became a Christian.

Under Will's spiritual mentoring and a continual

exposure to worship and teaching in a solid church, Geoff's internal priorities began to shift. He discovered an internal spiritual drive to bring the details of his life in line with what he was learning from God's Word. He found to his delight a natural hunger to do things that please God and an amazing and growing sensitivity to and rejection of actions and choices that were out of line with God's Word. No one handed him a set of rules. His past desires for drugs and alcohol drastically diminished. His hunger to live God's way increased. Past relationships that put him in situations he couldn't handle were set aside. They were replaced by relationships that challenged, encouraged, and taught him rather than reinforcing self-destructive behavior.

Gradually, every aspect of Geoff's life began to change under the impact of his new outlook. Work ethics, personal Bible study, budgeting priorities, time spent in prayer—all these became new central expressions in his life. He experienced setbacks and questions. It took him almost four years to get his personal finances in order. He discovered sin was still a problem. But he learned that there was help and hope. God was working. He became an avid reader of good books and a faithful student of God's Book. He became immersed in a process we will describe at length later, but underwent a preparation for maturity.

Now Geoff's focus transcends his own spiritual and emotional needs. He has become a younger Will South—a spiritual reproducer. He looks around at work and sees dozens of men who live what he used to live. And rising inside of himself he feels a compassion for these men that overwhelms him. He feels compelled to treat them, in as many ways as possible, the way he knows he was treated when he was lost. These men raise questions and challenge Geoff to learn. He knows that the frontiers of spiritual growth and learning are still before him. He's come a long distance, but he knows God has much more ahead for him. God sent Will South into his life at a critical moment. Geoff now asks God to send him into the lives of others the same way.

I've watched Geoff grow over the past decade. I've heard his questions, felt his struggles, cried with him in hard lessons, rejoiced in his victories. I've seen the changes. I know that God has worked His morphing wonder in my friend. Along the way, He brought a wonderful woman into Geoff's life. The personal transformation in his life is reflected in his family. The chaotic core of his life has been replaced with a deep sense of rightness with God. I'm overwhelmed by all that God has done in Geoff's life.

Perhaps because of where he started, the changes in Geoff are easy to identify. What's not so easy to explain is why they happened. When you hear about a life like Geoff's—with such definite and dramatic changes—there's a temptation to think, *Wow, that's really neat. There must be a special category of Christians who have these very dramatic life-change stories. That's not me. Does God like these people more than He likes the rest of us?* We tend to think it is abnormal, unusual, and not really possible for all of us. Nothing could be further from the truth! What happened to Geoff was normal. He's the first to report that while he was directly involved in every decision in his new life, the effects and the desire to make the right decision did not come from him alone. He realizes that God was actively bringing about transformation in his life. It didn't happen because he was smarter or more favored by God, or even because he tried harder than other Christians. **It happened because Geoff came to know, understand, and cooperate early in his Christian life with how God works in the holy transformation process.**

What does a changed life look like? It looks like a worm becoming a butterfly. It looks like a guy who was lost and alone becoming a guy who can lead someone else home. The details of a changed life may vary, but remember this—it is the norm, available to all believers, and something only God can do.

2
MORPHING IS
FOR EVERYONE!

EPHESIANS 4:1–6

Geoff's story brings up a key point: morphing is for everyone. This life-change from the inside out is something God wants to do for everyone—even you. Notice that Geoff's story wasn't about keeping a bunch of rules or trying hard to be good. Instead, it was about spiritual birth, a relationship, a new love, and then out of that love—change.

Second Corinthians 5:17 says, "If anyone is in Christ, he is a new creation; the old has gone, the new has come!" Don't miss the *anyone* in this verse. Morphing, or changing, isn't only for the spiritual elite. It's for every single person who has the Spirit of God living in his or her life. If you are "born from above," your life can change. In fact, that's exactly what the apostle Paul is going to explain in the extended passage we will explore in this book, Ephesians 4:1–32. Paul makes an announcement: "It's morphing time."

This passage makes clear that morphing is not only possible; it's normal, expected, and even commanded. Holy transformation is not something we simply hope will happen some day. It is God's clear desire for every believer. Unfortunately, the great majority of Christians do not understand what this involves, how it works out in daily living, or why morphing is an essential aspect of the Christian life.

THE CALL:
LET JESUS LIVE HIS LIFE IN YOU!

> As a prisoner for the Lord, then, I urge you to live a life worthy of the calling you have received. Be completely humble and gentle; be patient, bearing with one another in love. Make every effort to keep the unity of the Spirit through the bond of peace.
> EPHESIANS 4:1–3

Let's examine the call to morph as we find it in Ephesians 4:1. "As a prisoner for the Lord, I urge you to live a life worthy of the calling you have received." Literally, the phrase translates "to walk worthy of the calling by which you were called." What is that call? It refers to Christ's invitation for you to come into relationship with Him. You have been chosen. You are forgiven. All the qualities Paul described in the first three chapters of Ephesians—being redeemed, being sealed by the Spirit, receiving every spiritual blessing—all these belong to you. He says, "Now what I want you to do is live a life that matches who you *are* in Christ."

It's almost as if Paul has written, "I've just spent three chapters describing your legs; now it's time to walk." That's a helpful picture. Walking always starts with little steps. First, simply standing upright presents a challenge for a child. Then, coaxed and cheered on by Mom and Dad, she takes her first step. She leans forward and transfers the weight to the foot that she instinctively moves to catch herself. She's unsure what to do next, so she falls. She's going to fall the next time, too. In fact, she's going to fall many times before she walks across the room. In order to gain your balance to walk, you have to risk falling.

Spiritual growth is a parallel. You can grow so that who you are in Christ becomes who you are in your lifestyle. The process involves one step of faith followed by another step of faith, then another and another. Walking means you have to get out of your comfort zone and lose balance, regain balance, lose balance, regain balance. That child tottering across the living room gives us a great picture of what it means to walk with God. That's how it works.

Paul uses a powerful word to describe the walk —"worthy." The original word for worthy refers to an ancient method for measuring weight. This method involves a counterbalance much like a child's teeter-totter. Something is placed on one end of the beam. This word "worthy" means to add weight to the other end of the beam so that it's equal—to balance the scales. (We get our term *axis* from this Greek word.)

Paul says, in effect, "I beg you, as a prisoner of

the Lord. My imprisonment for sharing the gospel and caring for you gives me the right to ask this of you. I plead with you. I urge you." (The original tense of this verse has the force of a command.) "I want you, in light of all God has given you—who you are in Christ—to live it out in such a way that your beliefs match your behavior, so your creed matches your conduct." It's God's calling upon each one of us as His children to live out our faith in Christ with such consistency and integrity that it impacts our relationships, our money, our time, our speech, and even our secret motives and thoughts. He says, "Live out all that you already are in Christ. Let the outside of your life balance the inside of your life. Let the other end of the beam be made level, so that when someone looks at you, you reflect externally exactly who you are internally." That's the command. It's a call to morph: by faith, let Jesus live His life through you.

Unfortunately, it's in attempting to follow this command that many believers get into trouble. After learning that it is only by God's grace that we have entered into this new relationship with Christ, we tend to revert to some very bad thinking in our attempts to live out this new life.

Do you realize that some of us spend our entire lives trying to earn God's favor—even after we're Christians? The first two or three years after Christ became Lord of my life I knew I was forgiven. I believed the Spirit of God came into me. I knew I was going to go to heaven. But from all my background and early teaching, I was still operating with serious misunderstandings about God. Somehow growing up I came to believe, "God loves you when you're good, but God doesn't love you when you're bad. So you better be good to get Him to love you." That's bad theology! It's not biblical, and it's not true.

God's unconditional love and grace are not only the basis of our *salvation* but the foundation for our *transformation*. A healthy spiritual life is not about trying really hard to be good or straining to get disciplined to read your Bible and pray a little longer. Genuine spiritual transformation is not measured by our human attempts to "clean up the outside of our cup" (see Matthew 23:25). You haven't arrived spiritually when through your own self-effort you get really committed and give some of your time or some of your money to good causes. Life-change doesn't mean you just try to clean up your language. Holy transformation is not about keeping rules. You know what those efforts are? They're all merely religion—an attempt to meet God's standards with only human strength. That's not the Christian life.

The Christian life, in its essence, is realizing that you were once dead, but then God made you alive. Christ lives in you. Right now you possess all the spiritual blessings and power available for all eternity. By faith, Jesus can live His life out through you. That describes the core of the Christian life. Living this way is not an option. It's a command. We must become in our daily living who we already are in our relationship with Christ.

"But how?" you ask. "How do you do that? How does it really work?" Let's explore the process of holy transformation.

The Process: Practice Sacrificial
Other-Centered Relationships

You might expect Paul to start by giving us a list of things to *do* in order to experience holy transformation. That's not the way it works. When God, through His Spirit, wants to teach us how radical life-change occurs, He doesn't begin with activities. Instead, He begins with *relationships*. Notice how Paul begins to outline the process of holy transformation: "Be completely humble and gentle; be patient, bearing with one another in love. Make every effort to keep the unity of the Spirit through the bond of peace" (Ephesians 4:2–3). As you examine these verses, notice the four key words: *humble, gentle, patient,* and *bearing.* These are crucial attitudes. They are parts of the process God uses to morph your life and make you like Christ. You and I cannot be like Christ apart from these attitudes—humility, gentleness, patience, and bearing.

Now notice the phrase "make every effort." That's actually one word in the original language. It describes a practice or action to be taken. This morphing process occurs through our relationships with others and through some very specific responsibilities we must accept in order for change to happen.

Where Morphing Takes Place

Butterflies change in a cocoon. Christians change in a community. Both experience shelter. Both experience struggle. This is one of the most difficult concepts for American Christians to accept and integrate into their lifestyle. In other parts of the world people have a communal concept of life. Generations stay close or even live with one another. Not so with mainstream Americans. We've got that John Wayne mentality: "I can do it myself." The average American Christian brings that same mentality into his or her relationship with Christ. He or she thinks, "It's me, God, my Bible, and prayer. If I hang around other people, and we encourage each other—that's nice but not necessary." For American Christians, community is optional. That's not what the Bible teaches.

The Bible teaches that God brings about life-change through His Word and His Spirit in the context of sacrificial, other-centered relationships. Show me a believer who is not in deep, intentional, authentic relationships with other believers in some kind of small group, and I'll show you a Christian who isn't growing. If the goal of the small group—it could be called a family, a growth group, a ministry team, or a gathering of very close friends—includes meeting regularly, learning about the Scriptures, sharing what God is teaching the participants, and with intentionality speaking the truth into one another's lives, it will produce change. Those are people whose lives are morphing. You show me a Christian who is not involved in authentic community and I will show you a Christian who is not changing—period. No ifs, no ands, and no exceptions. Note that I didn't say their lives weren't filled with church activities, Bible reading, and ministry. I merely pointed out that their lives were not being supernaturally transformed by God's grace into more loving and holy people from the inside out.

Notice how every one of the four attitudes Paul mentions involves other people. The implications are obvious. I mean, how can you be humble alone? How can you be patient alone? How can you be gentle by yourself? How can you bear with when there's no one to bear with? Isn't it interesting that none of these attitudes can be developed in a vacuum? They require a community. The God of the Bible is the God who lives in relationships and who brings about holy transformation as we also live in relationship.

So, how about you? Do you have these kinds of relationships operating in your life? Are you involved in a small group (formally or informally) where you are sharing honestly what God is doing in your life? Do you have regular times with other believers where you pull back the masks that we all wear to one degree or another and really share your heart, your failures, your needs, and your dreams? If not, then you've just discovered one of the crucial reasons why spiritual transformation is not occurring in your life to the degree God intended. We tend to believe we can develop spiritually in isolation, but it doesn't work.

FOUR ATTITUDES

Let's look at the four attitudes that create the climate where life-change occurs.

Humility

Paul began his list of qualities with *humility,* which means "to have an accurate view of yourself." Humility is not feeling like you're a bad person or a small person, and it's not thinking that you're a big person or an important person. Humility is not thinking of yourself at all. Romans 12:3 says, "For by the grace given me I say to every one of you: Do not think of yourself more highly than you ought, but rather think of yourself with sober judgment, in accordance with the measure of faith God has given you." We need to evaluate accurately who we are based on the faith God gives us. Not falsely humble, but honestly recognizing what we bring to the table. We must also recognize what our deficits are. In essence, humility is a biblical, honest appraisal of ourselves. It means we come to relationships with a focus on others and not on ourselves.

It's easy to find people who are arrogant. Their pride is obvious. But other forms of pride abound that are frequently accepted in Christian circles. People who talk about themselves all the time or people who talk about their problems constantly or who can't seem to get beyond a victim mentality are all expressing subtle forms of pride. Who are they thinking about the whole time? Themselves. That's pride.

Paul shows us that transformation requires the practice of sacrificial, other-centered relationships— servanthood. In other words, humility has little to do with how you feel and a lot to do with where your focus is and how you treat others. Jesus left us a

beautiful example of this principle on the night before He was crucified. When He met with His disciples for what we call the Last Supper, He took off His
outer garment, wrapped a towel around His waist,
and washed their feet. He said, "Blessed are you, if
you understand—knowing who I am and what I
have just done—blessed are you if you do it to one
another" (see John 13:1–17). It's putting other people first—that's how you grow in Christ. It takes
practice. You have the power to do it because you're
in Christ, but it doesn't happen automatically.

When you, by faith, make a conscious effort out
of your love for Christ to serve others, you will discover that Jesus will begin to manifest His life and
power through you. But you will also discover that
being a servant will reveal some not-so-Christlike
attitudes in your heart. That highlights the importance of the next character trait that leads to holy
transformation. God's Spirit wants to help you develop gentleness.

Gentleness

The second morphing attitude is *gentleness*. It
means "to be considerate." It has the idea of restraint.
It's the concept of not having to have your own
rights. It's knowing the right answer and being able
to embarrass someone, but you think instead, "No,
I'm not going to go there." It's power under control.

When the mob came by night to arrest Jesus, He
went willingly. He could have called legions of angels
but He did not. When Pilate was in His face, Jesus

remained silent. When His accusers perjured themselves, and He could have crushed them, He did not object. (See Matthew 26:45–56, 59–63; 27:11–14.) That's gentleness. Did Jesus restrain Himself because He was weak? No. He held back because He was strong. He had nothing to prove, nothing to lose, no one to impress. Those who have morphed into Christlikeness will exercise remarkable gentleness in their dealings with others.

As you willfully choose to "give up" your rights in these relational situations, you will quickly discover a bruised ego dwelling within and a desire to tell others "how much you really know" or "what you could have done." Developing gentleness will drive you back to your identity in Christ. You will rest in the fact that you are secure, loved, valued, and already significant. You won't have to impress others, fight for approval, or try to get your own way. This "power under control" will allow you to identify and experience Christ's sufferings in some small way. It will also begin transforming deep identity issues that are foundational to holy transformation.

But, being human, you will at times cry out in your heart, *How long, Lord, do I have to put up with this?* That question leads us to the third and fourth attitudes.

Patience

Paul's third listed attitude is *patience.* It means steadfastness and suffering. It's the reluctance to take personal offense. It's being able, when another driver on the interstate gives you the finger or cuts in front of you, when everything in you wants to strike back, to say, "No." In fact, the Greek word is *makrothymia* (*macro,* a lot; *thymia,* heat). It's the idea of having a long, long fuse before you get angry.

Why? Because you don't have to get angry. You're in Christ. Someone else's evaluation of you or attack on you does not have the power to determine who you are or how you respond. People who get mad, who have to defend their rights, are people who down deep don't like themselves, are insecure, and don't understand that if they are in Christ they are already complete. So much of our lack of patience is simply pride rooted in our failure to accept that we don't need others' approval and we don't need to prove ourselves superior.

Bearing

Finally, *bearing with one another* literally means to put up with other people—their quirks, their failures, and their idiosyncrasies.

Even after we exercise humility, gentleness, and patience, some people will still simply require "putting up with." Why do it? Out of love for Christ, who puts up with them and with us. You see, morphing begins with understanding who we are in Christ (Ephesians chapters 1–3) and taking seriously God's command to let Jesus live out His life through us. The process occurs, not in a monastery or merely in our personal devotional life, but foremost in our relationships with others.

ONE PRACTICE

Having listed the underlying attitudes, Paul then says to "make every effort" (Ephesians 4:3), or take pains, be diligent, pay whatever price. He knew that morphing involved struggle. The call is to let Jesus live His life through you. The process is not easy. It's not getting any more of Jesus. It's Him getting more of you. You have begun to morph when you can say with your whole heart, "I'm going to learn to be a servant. I'm going to learn to be gentle and give up my rights. I'm going to learn to be patient and have a long fuse. I'm going to learn to bear with other people. I'm not going to hang around only with people I like and who make me feel good. I'm going to reach out to other kinds of people with whom I am uncomfortable, and I'm going to treat them as Jesus would treat them."

You see, to God morphing is not the stuff of an esoteric spiritual experience. Though we all long for special emotional experiences with God, the morphing process involves the application of objective truth in real-life relationships. And it is in the conscious, willful obedience to the above four attitudes that the Spirit of God begins to form the very character and nature of Christ in our lives. In that obedience we find our responsibility.

The text goes on to say clearly, "Make every effort to maintain [or keep] the unity." God's Word doesn't order us to *achieve* the unity; we already possess it. It says *maintain* the unity. Well, what unity is Paul talking about? Maintain the unity of the church, the relationships between you and God and between you and others. Why? To preserve "the unity of the Spirit through the bond of peace." We are believers. We need to reflect to one another how God loves and treats us. And so we are commanded, with these four attitudes, to treat one another the way God treats us. He's patient with you. He's patient with me. He puts up with my idiosyncrasies and He puts up with yours. The Spirit commands you and commands me to make every effort to exhibit the nature and the character of Christ to others in the same way that we have received it.

Although I have made a strong point that the Christian life is not about keeping rules or being religious, please don't confuse that with lack of effort. It is only by faith, through God's grace, that we enter a relationship with God. And it is only by faith, through God's grace, that holy transformation occurs. **However, many confuse the concept of grace with inactivity or lack of effort. This part of God's Word makes very clear that, once we understand who we are in Christ, there are specific attitudes that we must choose to practice, whether we feel like it or not.** We are commanded to make every effort to treat one another in the very way God treats us. It is through that obedience that the grace of God will manifest the power of the Holy Spirit to give you exactly what you need. As Paul would say if he were looking over your shoulder, "Morphing is happening inside you!"

Before we end this chapter, I want to emphasize one more point that I believe is imperative. It has to do with why morphing is so important. And before we address it, I simply want to say this:

- As much as you want to change, and

- as much as you know that genuine happiness and blessedness only occurs when your life is being conformed to the image of Christ, and

- as wonderful as the benefits of morphing are to those around you, the reason to morph is far greater than any personal reward you could ever receive.

WHY MORPHING MATTERS MORE THAN YOU THINK

There is one body and one Spirit—just as you were called to one hope when you were called—one Lord, one faith, one baptism; one God and Father of all, who is over all and through all and in all.
EPHESIANS 4:4–6

The call to morph, to life-change, to become like Christ, is far more important than you could ever dream. The ultimate purpose in God's goal of holy transformation for every believer becomes clear in Ephesians 4:4–6. God's Spirit put these statements together in a crescendo to a very significant point. At the end of that crescendo is the truth that morphing is absolutely imperative for every believer because God's church must reflect His character. Why?

The reason is this: "There is one body and one Spirit
—just as you were called to one hope when you were
called—one Lord, one faith, one baptism; one God
and Father of all, who is over all and through all and
in all" (Ephesians 4:4–6).

Actually, the phrase "there is" is not in the original text. Paul inserted no bridging words between the
phrase "the unity of the Spirit through the bond of
peace" and the next three verses. Literally, in the original text it just says, "the bond of peace; one body and
one Spirit." The grammar creates an emphatic connection between the Spirit's peaceful unifying effect
and the underlying spiritual reasons Paul lists next.

WHAT UNITY LOOKS LIKE

One body, one Spirit, one hope, one Lord, one
faith, one baptism, one God and Father—Paul provided seven staccato terms in Ephesians 4:4–6, giv-
en in triads, to outline the central unity of the body
of Christ. It's not hard to figure out what's going on
here. Each member of the Trinity receives specific attention. Seven times the word *one* is used. Four times
the word *all* is used. *One* emphasizes the unity; *all*
emphasizes the inclusion of everyone who is in
Christ and the absolute sovereignty of God.

The first triad includes one body, one Spirit, and
one hope. The one body refers to us—the church.
Who brought the church into existence and brings
each of us into it through Christ? The Holy Spirit.
What do we have in common as members of the one

body under one Spirit? The one hope that one day we will all be in heaven where we have been called.

The second triad centers on the Son. One Lord (Jesus), one faith (our trust in Him), and one baptism make up the threesome. The last of these is not so much the picture of water baptism as a reference to our shared identity—we have come into the church—through Jesus as Lord. We have one Lord. Our faith is rooted only in Him even as we are baptized into Him alone.

Paul closes the list with what could be called a sovereign summary: "One God and Father of all, who is over all and through all and in all" (Ephesians 4:6). This brief phrase manages to highlight both the divine nature and the personal character of God. He is God without equal or competitor. He is also Father, drawing close to us in love. So the sequence that begins with the unity of God the Spirit leads through the Lordship of Christ to the sovereignty of God the Father. He's over all. He's in all. He's through all. He's got your situation and every situation under control.

So, why did Paul add these two verses to his explanation of morphing? Because your transformation into the likeness of Christ and my transformation into the likeness of Christ is not simply about God's agenda or plan for us as individuals. As important as that may be, His overriding agenda is His agenda for His church and for His world. **When we begin to think that holy transformation is about us—our happiness, our fulfillment, our spiritual growth —we lose sight of the big picture.** The apostle Paul has pointed our attention to the theological Milky Way of God's greatness to remind you and to remind me that holy transformation is an imperative because your life is a mini-expression of the reality of Jesus Christ. Our lives together—the church—form a larger expression of the reality of God and His love for the world expressed by us individually.

So Paul, after telling us who we are in Christ for three chapters in Ephesians, commands us by the Spirit of God to morph, to enter into a process of relationships and attitudes in which this can occur. Now he has told us this is absolutely imperative because of what's at stake. The center of attention is not your devotional life or mine. What's at stake is not your happiness or mine. What is at stake is the very reality of the Godhead's unity expressed in and through this miraculous creation He calls the church.

If what you just read feels heavy, it is. When you look at the church in America and see the lack of holy transformation, is it any wonder that our culture raises the question "Is Christianity valid?" Is it any wonder that we have a hard time making our case for the reality of Christ and the gospel? After all, the lives of those who name the name of Christ are in large measure no different from those who don't.

This chapter ends with the statement with which we began, **"Morphing is for everyone!"** God has provided everything you and I need to become more and more like Jesus. This is not an option—it's a command.

This truth can make us feel uncomfortable or discouraged. It's possible to look in the spiritual mirror and realize that your life has not changed significantly since you came to Christ. There may be major areas that need to be addressed that you have attempted to change, but in your most honest moments you have to admit remain almost untouched by your best efforts. **Please do not despair.** There is hope. In the next chapter we will consider the three most common reasons why we fail to morph. Then, in the remaining chapters we will outline in practical terms how to be a part of God's miraculous process of holy transformation.

3
THREE REASONS
WE FAIL TO MORPH
"KEEPING THE UNITY OF THE SPIRIT THROUGH THE BOND OF PEACE"

For the first two years of my Christian life, I lived in two worlds. Thursday nights I was singing praises to God in the living room of a bricklayer who led our campus ministry. But Friday nights I was barhopping with my basketball team buddies all over downtown Wheeling, West Virginia.

I was a miserable hypocrite plagued by a never-ending cycle of failure, guilt, depression, repentance, resolutions to never do that again, another try, and back to failure again. I had tasted the reality and freedom of my new life in Christ, but living out that reality consistently seemed beyond my grasp. Fortunately for me, God brought some great people and some biblical teaching into my life that broke this vicious cycle. Unfortunately, that's not the case for many Christians today.

George Barna has done exhaustive studies of American Christians. The divorce rates among believers and nonbelievers are about the same. Involvement in pornography traps believers and nonbelievers in about the same numbers. Parenting problems plague families about equally inside and outside the church. Money matters seem to overwhelm believers and nonbelievers at about the same rate. The best research indicates that, among all the believers in America, only some 10 percent live out their faith in a way that really makes a difference in their lifestyle and values. The people who make up this 10 percent are not perfect, but, in the midst of all the normal struggles we all face in a fallen world, Christ owns their finances, He owns their relationships, He owns their time, and He owns their priorities. They parent His way, they relate His way, they are pure His way, and they are single His way. So only one out of ten Christians in America is actually, in the terms of this passage, maintaining "the unity of the Spirit through the bond of peace." Why is that?

One explanation is that actually living Jesus' way in a fallen world sure is hard, isn't it? At least it is for me. I admit it seems easier to stick with the 90 percent. The problem however, turns out to be even more complicated than laziness. I believe most Christians really want to change. Yet I meet countless Christians who struggle over *how* to change. They feel they are living a life of duplicity. I don't meet many people saying, "Yeah, I'm glad that I'm a Christian, but I'm going to live my own way and I don't care." If they didn't care at all, I'd question whether they were really in the family.

Instead, I meet a lot of sincere Christian people whose lives really don't reflect the Lord Jesus. They feel that they ought to, and they can describe attempts to live for Christ, all leading to failure. They say, "I know I should pray. I know I should be connected to other people. I know I have gifts and I know I'm not using them, but I'm so busy." Or "I know that living with my boyfriend is wrong, but I can't seem to make the break." Or even "I know my priorities are out of sync and I need to 'get back to God,' but there's so much to do. I feel so pulled in so many directions that I often just give up."

These statements sadden me but rarely surprise me, because I know how easily they can echo my own experience. However, God never intended those kinds of statements to be the norm, but only the exception for brief periods of time in our lives. So what keeps us from experiencing the supernatural changes commanded in Ephesians 4:1? Why is there so much desire to change among believers yet, honestly, so little genuine, sustained, positive morphing? The answer is threefold, and it flows right out of the text we have been studying.

THE FIRST REASON WE FAIL TO MORPH: SPIRITUAL IGNORANCE

Failure to morph frequently results from spiritual ignorance. Many Christians simply don't understand their identity in Christ and the grace they have received. That ignorance destines them to the "try hard, do good, fail" syndrome. My experience with the average believer is that he really doesn't know what it means to be "in Christ." Typical believers actually think they're in some sort of reward-and-good-deeds type of arrangement with God. They don't understand and often can't even articulate a definition of the word *justification*. The average Christian has no idea what actually happened to him the moment he received Christ. He is not stunned by the fact that he was justified.

We are living today in an age of biblical illiteracy, and we are paying the price for it with confused and shallow spiritual lives. As you read the following few paragraphs, please ask God to help you begin to understand what actually occurred in you the moment you placed your faith in Christ. Remember what Jesus said: "You will know the truth, and the truth will set you free" (John 8:32).

Justification is a theological word. You can find it in the Bible (see, for example, Acts 13:39; Romans 3:24, 28; 4:25; Galatians 2:16–17; Titus 3:7). The biblical word *justification* simply means that God takes all the sin and guilt in the debt column in your life (that you justly owe to a holy God) and makes every item on that list "paid in full." God does this on the basis of what Christ did on the cross. At the moment you received Christ, God removed all the legal debt and penalty for the sin that separated you from Him. In addition to that, He took the righteousness of Christ and *imputed* (deposited) it to your account, so that your position before God for all eternity is pure and holy in His sight. You are "in Christ." You are justified—or just-as-if-I'd-never-sinned. Your sins are removed and replaced by Christ's righteousness. That's your legal standing before God. That's how God, the divine judge, sees you. You don't live trying to *get* that. You live out of the reality of *having* it. You've got it. It's a gift called grace.

Christians are often spiritually ignorant about the process of holy transformation. They don't know how to grow spiritually. Or, to use the word we described above, they don't know how to live out of their justification. In order to do so, we need to understand another rich, theological, biblical word: *sanctification.* That big word matches the large process it describes (see, for example, John 17:17; Romans 15:16; 1 Thessalonians 4:3; 5:23). It simply means "being set apart." It's the process by which, over time, God changes your heart and life from the inside out to conform your character to the image of His Son (Romans 8:29). Christians who begin to grasp what it means to be justified in Christ usually start asking pressing questions:

- How do you make use of the grace that you possess?
- How do you appropriate this new life and relationship with God Monday through Saturday at home and at work?
- Why do I "keep sinning" if God forgave all my sins when I came to Christ?
- How do you live a holy life in a sin-saturated society?

Sadly, many believers don't know how to answer those questions. So they tend to do the same thing I did the first couple of years I was a Christian. Maybe you are familiar with this cycle. You start with the "try hard, do good, fail; try hard, do good, fail; try hard, do good, fail" routine. Pretty soon that becomes the "try hard sort of, do good, fake it" approach. This leads to the "don't try so hard, can't do good, fake it even more" desperation. Eventually the repeated process gets shortened to "try hard, quit." The vicious cycle loses its humor when we plug in the real issues we deal with during these frustrating efforts. Does this sound familiar?

- "I'm trying hard to read my Bible. I read a little last week. I can't get it."

- "I'm trying to conquer my sexual lusts. I can't stop them. They're back."

- "I've been trying hard to pray. The answers don't seem clear. I skipped again today."

- "I'm sick of 'blowing up' at my mate. I'm trying to change, but it never lasts!"

This pattern of trying hard, then doing well, then failing can be devastating. Some eighteen months into my Christian life I was so exasperated with my continued failures that I seriously considered quitting the Christian life. Little did I know that it was my lack of knowledge about God, His Word, and the sanctification process that destined me to this vicious cycle of spiritual failure. If we don't learn how to tap into God's grace and power for living, we remain in spiritual ignorance. I honestly believe that massive numbers of believers all over America are living defeated, un-Christlike lives because they simply don't know or understand what God's Word teaches about holy transformation.

Spiritual ignorance also shows up in our inability to live out what the Bible calls "walking by faith." We don't know enough of the Bible to know how to respond to issues in life by applying God's Word. Walking by faith involves "life alerts" from Scripture. As God's Word reveals a problem in us, we begin to talk with Him and realize this is an issue we have to resolve. We ask the question, "What does it look like to trust God in this situation, relationship, or financial difficulty?" We then take our focus off the problem and by faith trust the promises from God's Word that apply to our situation. We make decisions based on God and His promises to us. It's called **walking by faith** and it is at the core of all Christian living. This is not as mystical as it sounds. In fact, let me show you what it looks like in real life.

We take a step of faith by sharing our need in community with other brothers and sisters in humility, patience, and longsuffering, making every effort to maintain unity in the Spirit by adressing an area of sin in our lives. God uses their gifts, knowledge, and experience to help us learn how to trust Him. As a group, together we overcome the issues in our lives, because God gives grace through His Word, His Spirit, and His people. In this process we realize *I'm totally loved, I'm totally accepted, but I long to be pleasing to my God. And now I'm living out my faith the same way I got saved—by faith, through grace.*

The remedy for spiritual ignorance is simple, and obvious, but profound. We must master the English Bible. I don't mean, "Read the Bible a little here and a little there." I don't mean, "Glance at a chapter now and then, or read a devotional." I mean, **"One of your life goals as a believer is to master the contents and doctrine of the English Bible."** Before you roll your eyes at me and tell me how impractical that is, let me ask you how often you catch the nightly news? My guess is that you spend thirty to ninety minutes each day just keeping up with what's going on in the world. Imagine taking half that time and systematically reading through the Bible daily. Now widen that to include not only reading your Bible but also reading a few basic study helps that would define the major doctrines of the Bible and a few key books that would help you grow spiritually. Imagine sharing what you are learning with a small group once a week or once every other week. The results would be staggering, for you would not merely be "taking in knowledge about God" but would be beginning to put it into practice and pass it on to fellow believers. I guarantee that if you exchanged your "daily news intake" for a three-month commitment to "master the English Bible" in the way I've just described, your life would be revolutionized.

If this sounds a bit strange, it shouldn't. The problem is what has happened to us as Christians in our culture today. It's not with God, His truth, or how life-change actually occurs. During the time of Christ, the average Jewish boy memorized the entire Pentateuch (the first five books of the Bible). Imagine what would happen to you if you memorized only one or two verses *a week,* choosing passages that related to the biggest issues that you were struggling with. Imagine being able to read through the book of John or Mark or First Thessalonians, and being able to think your way through them chapter by chapter, building up a reservoir of truth that would help you deal with life's most complex problems and relationships.

Get the idea? This will obviously not happen overnight. But it could certainly begin today! If you want a life that morphs—a life characterized by holy transformation—it will require that you become a person of the Book. There are no shortcuts! Spiritual ignorance is lethal. God wants far better for you and for me.

The Second Reason We Fail to Morph: Spiritual Isolation and Failure to Form Christ-Centered, Honest Relationships

A second reason we fail to morph is spiritual isolation, or failure to actively involve ourselves with in-depth, Christ-centered, honest relationships. Remember: We learned that a butterfly is transformed in a *cocoon,* but a Christian is transformed in a *community.* Let me say this emphatically: **You will never experience holy transformation until you are involved in regular, loving, accountability relationships centered on God's Word.** So what do these relationships look like and how do they work?

Well, if you're in a family and you happen to be the father, you need to get out the Bible at least once or twice a week and read a little section systematically and talk about it with your kids. You don't have to be an expert and you don't have to answer all their questions. But you can model that God's Word is important, and you can teach them the basics of the Christian life. Make those times brief, fun, and focused on application, not information. There are many excellent resources to help you in this area. Walk Thru the Bible ministry has a monthly family devotional publication called *Family Walk* that provides everything you need for effective family times at very low cost. (Check them out at www.WalkThruTheBible.org.) If your children are small, get some good Bible storybooks and read them at bedtime. Your family is the most important small group God ever designed.

If you're a single parent, the paragraph you just read may seem or feel almost impossible. You come home tired, and it takes an extraordinary amount of energy to create regular times in God's Word for you and your children. Let me encourage you to find the support of other single parents and some married couples to help you in this venture. Part of the answer may be a small group where you can lean on one another and hold each other accountable for regular times of honest prayer and Bible content in your homes. Holy transformation demands this kind of spiritual connectedness from the heart around God's Word.

It may surprise you, but the hidden cause behind spiritual isolation is pride. Now, I don't mean the "puff out your chest, I don't need anybody or anything" kind of pride. I'm talking about the kind of pride that is subtle and insidious. It's the kind of pride that unconsciously thinks, *My life and my agenda are more important than God's.* It's pride revealed not by our words but by our behavior that says, *My work, my fun, my stuff, my priorities are more important than getting into God's Word and being connected to other believers.* This results in a lack of deep relationships with other believers and, over time, an unwillingness to serve them. That's what the Bible calls pride. It's the lack of a servant's heart. It's being duped by our culture into thinking that if you can just get enough stuff and have enough fun and make enough money and live in the right place, then you'll be happy.

Our world is overrun by a whole generation of people who have reached the pinnacle of success yet are on medication for their depression. They've got "everything"—everything but meaningful relationships. My point boils down to this: Being in a small group or a ministry team isn't just a "nice option" in life. Having a few close friends where you share your heart and your life at the deepest level, centered on the Scriptures, doesn't represent a "nice idea." These are *core components* of healthy life. They are the prerequisites for holy transformation to occur. You will be a stagnant, status quo, "90 percent of the believers in America" kind of Christian unless you're in a functioning small group, ministry team, or family relationship where you practice humility, patience, gentleness, and bearing with each other for the expressed purpose of mutually becoming like Christ. Where else can you open your life and ask, "Would you help me become like Jesus?"

I can tell you that the people who have had the

greatest impact on my life are people that have spoken truth into my life. They've loved me enough to say, "Chip, you are arrogant," or "Chip, you are insensitive," or "Chip, you are treating Theresa (my wife) in a way that's going to be bad news in five years," or "Chip, you are way too hard on your kids." That kind of hard but loving comment has spared me untold heartache, but they are not the kinds of words you hear from strangers or casual acquaintances. Deep, honest, vulnerable relationships take time, intentionality, and effort. As a result, I believe I continually have to be in some type of growth group.

I don't know what you are doing in your life, but apart from eating, sleeping, making a living, and parental responsibilities, a growth group experience is more important than anything else you can do. You won't change without it. I mean, that's Jesus' example. Do you think it was accidental that when Jesus wanted to transform the world He didn't set up a classroom, write a book, or develop a video seminar? He didn't say, "OK, guys, I'm God. Just thought I'd show up. I've got a game plan for the world. Class will be in session at nine o'clock tomorrow morning. See you then." He didn't do that. Instead, He started a small group and had them live with Him.

The Navigator who discipled me—I lived with him. How did I learn about marriage? I watched his marriage. You know how I learned about parenting? I watched him parent his kids. I learned about stopping in the middle of a rainy day and changing the tire of some broken-down car when I saw him do that as the leaders of a conference we'd just left all drove on by. I learned servanthood by watching him serve. I knew what he taught me was true because his life illustrated his message. I know from my own experience that more truth is caught than taught in relationships. You must be connected to other people, or you will not change.

THE THIRD REASON WE FAIL TO MORPH:
SPIRITUAL MYOPIA

Spiritual myopia describes the third reason many fail to change. This theological problem becomes apparent when we fail to see the magnitude of what is at stake in our call to Christlike behavior. This condition minimizes the importance of our character development and shatters our motivation. *Myopia,* the inability to see clearly or rightly, describes the failure to see the value of what's at stake in our call to balance the scales between who we are in Christ and how we actually live. Most of us think that we should be more like Christ because we feel guilty when we're not. Most of us think it's important because we would be happier and more fulfilled and God might use us more. Those concerns serve as nice little motivations. But they are not the right motivation. They are not big enough or high enough from God's perspective!

Here's what's at stake, according to this passage, when my life doesn't reflect what I say I believe. My life becomes a walking billboard that proclaims, "Not one body, not one Spirit, not one hope, not one Lord, not one faith, not one baptism. Not one God. Not one Father." If all those "ones" are real, then my life needs to reflect what's actually true. Spiritual myopia can't see that big-picture reasoning.

It is a subtle, insidious disease that makes spiritual progress merely a personal matter and one that's no one else's business but mine. Yet based on what they see in the lives of Christians, people out there are wondering, *Is the church real? Is the Spirit of God real? Is heaven real? Does hope exist? Is God the Father real? Is He sovereign? Is Jesus Lord?* The most convincing evidence is not our apologetics but our lifestyle. The apostle Paul tells us that when we live a selfish, self-centered, me first, "my way" life, we discredit the person of God, the person of Christ, and the church.

No wonder 25 percent of people in America say they're born again, yet our culture has the highest violence and murder rates in the world. The salt has lost its saltiness. The light shines only dimly, because we think genuine spiritual change is an option. We have accepted the culture of consumerism. Christianity has been reduced to a list of how-to's: how to have a happy life, how to have a wonderful marriage, how to have your kids turn out right, and how to do well in business and love God at the same time. All those are nice by-products, but not the call of God. The call of God is "There is one body (you, me, the church), there is one Spirit supernaturally working, there is one hope—we're made for heaven, and this world is not our home."

The remedy for spiritual myopia is to get a high view of God. We've got to come back to biblical

Christianity, and that means we return to His Word. It means we read people like A. W. Tozer (*Knowledge of the Holy*) and J. I. Packer (*Knowing God*).[1] It means we turn off the tube, shut off the PlayStation, and begin reading about, thinking about, and discussing what we're learning about God. We ask and express our answers to life's deepest questions: *Why are we here? What really matters?* You and I have been dumbed-down for so many years that we avoid anything that's hard or stretches us—anything that takes real concentration. It's time to give your brain a workout. Let your mind expand. Get an accurate and renewed view of God. Memorize a classic passage, such as Isaiah 40 or Psalm 145. Read J. P. Moreland's book *Love God with All Your Mind*.[2] But be careful. You may find a new motivation and zeal begin to spring up in your heart. Your prayers will deepen and your joy will increase. You might get outside your culture and say, "Man, this is a mess." Great thinking always begins with great reading. Study God's holiness. Practice loving God with all your mind.

CONCLUSION

Which of the three hindrances to life-change do you most closely identify with in this chapter? Is it spiritual ignorance—you just don't really understand who you are in Christ or how to appropriate your spiritual identity? Is it spiritual isolation—are you functionally, practically isolated from other believers? Or is it spiritual myopia—have you somehow been squeezed (this happens to me over and over) into the world's thinking that as long as this Christianity works for me (that's pragmatism) then I must be doing OK?

Well, I've got news for you. The issue isn't whether or not Christianity works. The issue is whether or not you and I are obedient to the holy, omnipresent, all-powerful God, who's got an agenda for the planet and an agenda for us. **Holy transformation requires biblical knowledge, authentic community, and a high view of God.** God's work in our lives is a miraculous work of grace. But in His wisdom and sovereignty He allows us, even commands us, to be highly engaged in this process of transformation. He wants you and me to "make every effort" to live out what He has deposited within us.

So, how about you? Where do you go from here? Which one of those obstacles is most prominent in your life? What is keeping you from holy transformation? What specific step do you think you ought to take to remove one of the hindrances we talked about in this chapter? Begin by saying to God, "I want to morph out of spiritual ignorance, or spiritual isolation, or spiritual myopia into someone who obeys You in each of these areas." Remember: You don't need any more of God. If you are a believer, you already have all that you'll ever need of Him. What you need to learn is how to tap it. And that's what we're going to talk about in the next chapter— how to experience the power to do exactly what we have just talked about.

4

THE KEY TO MORPHING: LIFE-CHANGE . . .

IT CAN HAPPEN TO YOU

EPHESIANS 4:7–10

Morphing presents us with an all-or-nothing proposition. It can be a little overwhelming. The caterpillar doesn't get to try one wing on for size just to see if he's all right with metamorphosis. Cocoons require total commitment. People talk about wanting to change, but when a genuine opportunity comes along they often decide to wait. I've known many alcoholics who swear they are going to quit drinking once and for all, right after the next drink. I've known even more Christians who weep and agonize over the changes they tell me they want to experience in their lives and yet they remain the same, year after year. On the other hand, I've also watched some very unlikely candidates bound so deeply in sinful behaviors that their escape was humanly impossible, yet they were freed to fly. And I've seen regular people, like you and me, with unspectacular sins and unremarkable character become unexpectedly effective in the body of

Christ. Their transformation has been as startling and colorful as the change from a caterpillar to a butterfly. I believe this can happen to you.

FACING OUR BIGGEST
CHALLENGE HEAD-ON!

I said in the last paragraph that I believe this kind of holy transformation can happen in your life. I've seen it happen repeatedly in mine. I've watched it happen in others' lives. But truthfully, it doesn't happen often enough and, when it does, it involves a significant struggle. Let's let the cat out of the bag and talk frankly about the biggest challenge that keeps us from continually experiencing morphing. The answer is pretty simple—it's sin! What keeps me from becoming like Jesus is sin. When I'm selfish, when I'm envious, when I'm lustful, when I demand my own way, and when I hurt other people, it's sin. When I do the right things for the wrong reasons— to please people, to impress others, or to simply gain attention and affirmation for me—it's sin. The action may look good on the outside, but it's wrong and it's sin. My flesh is in control, and I'm not experiencing the holy transformation God intended for me. Instead of the Spirit's being in control, helping me live out my new identity in Christ, I've allowed my flesh to be controlled by the impulses of sin. So the real question in morphing turns out to be, **How do you deal with the problem of sin?**

In this next section of Ephesians 4, Paul will take us on one of the most interesting journeys in all of the New Testament. It parallels his teaching in Romans 6:1–4, where he explains that continuing to live in sin is not an option for a Christian. And then he tells us why—because we have died to sin. He says, "Don't you know that all of us who were baptized into Christ Jesus [have been fully identified with Him] were baptized into his death?" (v. 3). In other words, in our new identity in Christ that has come by our faith in Jesus, we literally died with Christ. We died so that we could be resurrected with Christ and "walk in newness of life" (v. 4 NASB). Paul is teaching us that we can never live the resurrected life until we understand and accept that we have already died with Christ.

Stay with me here. I know this can get a little confusing. Breaking the penalty and the power of sin demands a clear understanding of what it means to die with Christ. In fact, Jesus used this exact parallel when He explained the spiritual life to His followers. In John 12:24–25 Jesus said, "I tell you the truth, unless a kernel of wheat falls to the ground and dies, it remains only a single seed. But if it dies, it produces many seeds. The man who loves his life will lose it, while the man who hates his life in this world will keep it for eternal life." Jesus was reminding His followers that a resurrection life must always be preceded by death. It's also important to remember that those of us who are in Christ have an entirely different view of death than those who don't know Him. For those in the world, death is a period; for us, it's a comma. It isn't the end, but a new beginning. Just like morphing.

We believe that Jesus not only conquered the penalty of sin, the power of sin, and the works of the devil, but He also conquered death when He died upon the cross and was resurrected. In fact, every Easter Sunday we celebrate His resurrection. But that resurrection would have been impossible unless He actually died.

Understanding what it means to be identified with Jesus' death is absolutely critical for the morphing process. It's so critical that the apostle Paul, in Ephesians 4:7–10, explains exactly what Jesus was actually doing between the time that He died on the cross and when He rose triumphantly from the grave. It may seem odd to us, but the apostle Paul uses the vivid language of ancient warfare to help us grasp the truth of Jesus' victory over death, sin, and the devil. The background of Paul's language is so fascinating that we can easily get lost in the historical panorama and graphic details and forget Paul's central purpose. In the next few pages we will answer the critical question raised by these verses: **What was Jesus doing between the time that He died and the time that He was resurrected?**

Please remember that the answer to this question isn't an end in itself. The Spirit's ultimate goal in this passage is for you to:

- understand what Jesus accomplished in His death, so that you can then
- grasp with your heart, mind, and soul that whatever He did in His death applies not only to Him but now also to you.

In other words, when you can grasp what Jesus' death actually accomplished with regard to your sin, to death, and to the works of our enemy the devil, you will be able to appropriate the grace that is already available for you to face those same opponents. You will actually be able to see sin, temptations, and the enemy of your soul not as potent and unbeatable foes threatening to overwhelm you but as completely humiliated and defeated enemies. Because of what Jesus did on the cross and beyond, you will, by grace, be able to overcome the power of sin, the flesh, and the devil in your life. The implications are the key to breaking the power of sin in our personal lives.

With that hopeful purpose in view, let's take the next leg of this spiritual journey together. What we are learning will help us understand what it means to die with Christ. We claim the great promise in Romans 8:11, "And if the Spirit of him who raised Jesus from the dead is living in you, he who raised Christ from the dead will also give life to your mortal bodies through his Spirit, who lives in you." The power that raised Jesus is the same power available for our holy transformation. "In the same way," Paul tells us, "count yourselves dead to sin but alive to God in Christ Jesus" (Romans 6:11). The morphed life is a life of righteousness.

A GLIMPSE BEYOND THE GRAVE

Here is the text of Ephesians 4:7–10:

> But to each one of us grace has been given as Christ apportioned it. This is why it says:

> "When he ascended on high,
> he led captives in his train
> and gave gifts to men."
>
> (What does "he ascended" mean except that he also descended to the lower, earthly regions? He who descended is the very one who ascended higher than all the heavens, in order to fill the whole universe.)

The gospel that ends with the Resurrection and the Ascension begins with the Incarnation. It's the story of God coming to the earth—fully man, yet still fully God. He lived a perfect life, taught truth, did miracles, communicated the way to have a relationship with God, and died on a cross to pay for our sin. Then He was raised the third day, all to demonstrate that God's love and Word are absolutely true. For forty days over five hundred eyewitnesses experienced the resurrected Lord in space-time history. That was God's visit to His own creation.

The result was a command by our resurrected Lord to go to the whole world to tell all people, "Here's the happy news! You're forgiven already. It's been done. Repent and receive the gift." That's the Easter story as we usually tell it. Those are the gospel highlights. They are often enough to bring people to faith in Christ. In fact, your own encounter with Jesus Christ (if it has already happened) may have involved only a simple message about God's love, Christ's death for sin, and your opportunity for response. That's enough for your spiritual birth to occur. But there is far more to the story.

We have much to learn once we are born into God's family. Every aspect of Jesus' life becomes a source for spiritual insights. In Ephesians 4:7–10, Paul provides a summary answer to our questions about what exactly was going on between the time that Jesus died and the time that He rose.

A CLOSER LOOK

Let's work through this text, phrase by phrase, to discover what Jesus was doing during those eventful hours between Friday afternoon and Resurrection Sunday morning. Verse 7 and the first words of 8 say, "But to each one of us grace was given according to the measure of Christ's gift. Therefore it says," (NASB). Paul makes a statement about the "grace" we have been given and measures its amount in relationship to Christ's generosity. The word "Therefore" introduces an Old Testament quote but also tells us that whatever we're going to learn in the next three verses includes an explanation of why believers in Jesus Christ have supernatural endowments or spiritual gifts in order to serve one another.

Paul then quotes an obscure passage from Psalm 68, "When He ascended on high, He led captive a host of captives, and He gave gifts to men" (Ephesians 4:8b NASB). In order to clarify his application of this Old Testament reference, Paul changes the person from "You ascended . . . you led . . . you gave," to its New Testament form. He's going to explain how we as believers came to receive spiritual gifts and why they are such a significant reminder of our new identity in Christ. In order to do this, he's going to give us some insight into events in the spiritual realm that we rarely think about.

Verse 9 says, "Now this expression, 'He ascended,' what does it mean except that He also had descended into the lower parts of the earth?" (NASB). The term "lower parts" refers to Hades, or Sheol, the Old Testament concept of the place of the dead. Paul goes on to say in verse 10, "He who descended is Himself also He who ascended far above all the heavens [here's the purpose], so that He might fill all things" (NASB).

The teaching in this passage requires that we do a little theological, historical, and cultural work. Why does Paul quote this Old Testament passage? What does it mean? How does it tie in with some other difficult passages?

What Christ Did

The first key phrase comes from verse 8, "He led captive a host of captives" (NASB). I don't know about you, but when I read this through the first time it didn't ring my bell. I mean, I didn't immediately think, *Oh, I know what that means.* But for a person during biblical times, and especially for a Jew, these words had a very precise meaning. During the time that Psalm 68 was written, Israel's enemies were severely oppressing her. The people cried out to God, and Psalm 68 is a picture of God coming in His power and His glory and beginning to wipe out the enemies of Israel. The psalm includes some vivid military imagery of the day.

When nations waged war in ancient times, battles often involved an attacking army pitted against a fortified city. The people of a city hunkered down behind towering walls and reinforced gates. The attackers surrounded the city and began building great earthen mounds against the walls. If they couldn't break or burn through the massive wooden doors, they eventually gained access to the city when the constructed ramps reached the top of the walls. Then they conquered the city and made captives of the people. Citizens became slaves and their possessions became the booty of the conquering army.

After a great victory, armies usually followed a certain protocol. The king or military leader got credit for the victory. This is exactly what occurs in 2 Samuel 12:27–31 when Joab leads David's army in battle against Rabbah. Shortly before the final victory, the general sent word to the king to come in order to claim the city. The details of such a conquest help us understand what Jesus accomplished during His days in the grave.

Once the city was captured, the king or the general would often ride a white horse as he returned from the conquered city back to his home city. The Romans even had a special word for this procession —*triumph*. Behind him marched all of his troops in shining battle array as the victors. Behind them, lined up in formation, three, four, or five abreast and often a mile or two long, depending on the number of captives, would be the conquered. The ancient world often practiced crude customs. The exhibition of captured prisoners represents a clear case in point. Some extrabiblical sources offer us appalling graphic descriptions of these marches. Captives had no rights. They were often partially or completely stripped of clothing and dignity while they were paraded as trophies of war. Victors utterly humiliated their foes.

Picture this vivid scene. Crowds cheer as the king enters his city with his army. Behind them trudges the dejected train of captives, heads bent to avoid eye contact with the onlookers. Behind them come the oxen, cattle, and the wagon loads of booty from their city. Those in chains know their defeat has been complete. Their city has been looted. Every gold, silver, jewel or valuable article is now someone else's property. The weeping of the victims is drowned out by the shouts of the crowd, heaping praise and honor on the king. Once the king arrives at his palace, the next order of business involves the sharing of the spoils. Everyone walks away from the parade with a valuable token of the king's victory. The gifts of oxen, jewelry, coins, and clothes taken from the captives were a constant reminder of the great victory over a formidable foe.

The apostle Paul is using this imagery to say, "If you want to understand why people who know Christ personally are given spiritual gifts, the reason is that Jesus won a battle. He won a battle over sin, over death, and over our enemy Satan. The proof of that victory lies in the spoils. And the spoils or the gifts are spiritual ones that He gives to His church." Now, that gives us a picture of what was going on in the spiritual realm while Jesus was dead—He defeated Satan's kingdom.

Where He Did It

The second key phrase or word is "the lower parts of the earth" (Ephesians 4:9 NASB). That language strikes us as strange. He has used one ancient picture to tell us what Christ did; now he's going to tell us where he did it. "Lower parts of the earth" alludes to Hades, or Sheol. In the Jewish mind-set, the afterlife was called Hades, or Sheol, and it had two major compartments. One area was the destination of the wicked dead, and the other was the destination of the righteous. In Luke 16:19–31, Jesus tells a parable that uses this framework of the afterlife. Most people remember it as the parable of Lazarus and the rich man. One lived in luxury while the other (Lazarus) lay sick and starving, wishing for the scraps from the rich man's table. After they died, the rich man went to the abode of the wicked and Lazarus went to paradise, or Abraham's bosom. In Jesus' description of the destination of these two men, a great chasm separates the two, though they can see each other. The details of Jesus' parable are consistent with the Jewish view of what occurs to Old Testament saints and to the wicked after death.

The apostle Peter, in 1 Peter 3:18–19, helps to further clarify Jesus' activities between His death and His resurrection. He went first to the punishment compartment of Hades. Peter writes, "For Christ died for sins [the context is Him dying on the cross] once for all, the righteous for the unrighteous, to bring you to God" (v. 18). Now notice the next part of verse 18 and all of 19: "He was put to death in the body [crucified on the cross] but made alive by the Spirit [resurrected], through whom [through the Spirit] also he went and preached to the spirits in prison." The Apostles' Creed of the early church talks about Jesus descending into hell. Now the word "preached" here does not refer to preaching the gospel so that the hearers might repent and be saved—these hearers are demonic forces. This preaching is a word for proclamation, a royal announcement. Jesus cried, "It is finished," on the cross for all the world to hear; then He went to Hades and proclaimed "The victory was won when I died on the cross. Sin's power has been broken. Death no longer has its sting, and you are a defeated foe."

Jesus also visited the paradise compartment of Hades that is the abode of Old Testament saints. This part of Jesus' pre-resurrection activities is mentioned in 1 Peter 4:6, "For this is the reason [speaking of what was occurring at the time] the gospel was preached even to those who are now dead." To whom does the phrase "those who are now dead" refer? They're the saints, the Old Testament believers. Peter continues, "So that they might be judged according to men in regard to the body, but live according to God with regard to the spirit." Jesus went to those Old Testament saints and He preached, but not the same message He delivered to the rebels in the other compartment. This word "preached" comes from a different Greek word than the word "preached" in 1 Peter 3:19. This is the word for the gospel—the good news. Jesus visited paradise to inform and confirm the faith of the Old Testament saints.

Every believer, of every time period in history (even before Christ) is saved on the same basis, the work of Christ. The Old Testament believers were looking forward in faith, much the same way that we look back in faith. They believed, "One day there will be a Messiah, a final sacrifice, and we will be forgiven based on that."

We believe, "The Messiah did come, a final sacrifice, and we are forgiven based on what He did." The Old Testament saints offered animal sacrifices each year on the Day of Atonement to remind them that there was yet no permanent payment for sin but that one day the Messiah would do that. The content of their faith was the truth about the just and forgiving character of God that they knew and lived by. The basis was the future work of Christ.

We are now on the other side of the Cross and we look back to the Cross as a finished work. The content of our faith is that Jesus died for us and rose again. And so Jesus, from the time that He died until He was resurrected, went to paradise for all those Old Testament saints. He told them, "I'm the Messiah; the work has been completed. God has accomplished what He promised to you."

Witness from the Cross

Remember the thieves on the crosses beside Jesus? One of them said, "We are punished justly, for we are getting what our deeds deserve—but he didn't do anything wrong" (see Luke 23:32–43). Then he cried out in faith to Jesus. Jesus said to him, "Today you will be with me in paradise" (v. 43). That thief died, and because of his faith in Christ he went to the paradise compartment, probably the last Old Testament saint. Now, what does this have to do with us today?

Why Christ Did It

Passages such as Hebrews 9:1–14, 22–28 make clear that nothing about Jesus' life occurred by accident. He lived in full cooperation with His heavenly Father's plans. His life, death, and resurrection provided the central piece in a puzzle that had been forming for centuries. Everything God did before that event in history prepared for it; everything God has done since has prepared for Christ's ultimate revelation as Lord of Lords and King of Kings (see Philippians 2:5–11). He is the once-and-for-all sacrifice. He is our great High Priest, and there is no more need for any high priests or sacrifices because of what He's done.

All of which brings us to the last phrase in our Ephesians passage: "That He might fill all things" (Ephesians 4:10b NASB). Jesus came to demonstrate what was always true—He is Lord. In other words, Jesus visited even the most godforsaken piece of real estate in creation that He might claim full control; that He might be recognized as the ruler, the sovereign, the deliverer of all the world and all the universe, including that which can be seen and that which cannot be seen. One passage in the New Testament reflects Christ's motivation in a powerful way. It's a picture of a heavenly celebration. John describes an amazing scene of multitudes honoring Jesus. He's called the Lamb who is worthy, the Lamb who was slain. This passage is Revelation 5:9–13.

And they sang a new song:

"You are worthy to take the scroll
and to open its seals,
because you were slain,
and with your blood you purchased men for God
from every tribe and language and people and
nation.
You have made them to be a kingdom and priests
to serve our God,
and they will reign on the earth."

Then I looked and heard the voice of many angels, numbering thousands upon thousands, and ten thousand times ten thousand. They encircled the throne and the living creatures and the elders. In a loud voice they sang:

"Worthy is the Lamb, who was slain,
to receive power and wealth and wisdom and
strength and honor and glory and praise!"

Then I heard every creature in heaven and on earth and under the earth and on the sea, and all that is in them, singing:

"To him who sits on the throne and to the Lamb
be praise and honor and glory and power,
for ever and ever!"

Jesus is the sovereign king, ruler, and deliverer of the universe.

So what does that mean to us? What was Jesus doing between the time of His death on the cross and the moment of His resurrection? The answer is profound and yet simple. **He was establishing His right to reclaim creation. He was declaring that He had defeated sin, death, and Satan. He was, in space-time, objective history, providing the basis for your spiritual freedom and transformation.** You see, we must remember that we are able to be transformed because we have died with Him. Having died with Him, we know that the penalty of sin has been broken once and for all, and the power of sin has been broken in its reigning control over our lives. The Enemy is now a defeated foe, subject to the authority of the Spirit of Christ and the Word of God dwelling within us.

These bedrock, objective truths are not intended to simply provide a fascinating theological discussion. Nor are they meant to merely challenge your attention span. They are crucial. I cannot overemphasize how important it is for you to grasp and understand the fact that dying with Christ is not merely a theological concept. You were and are organically connected to the Lord Jesus in such a way that when you accepted Him as your Savior, you died with Him. Therefore, all the benefits of His death and His victory over sin, death, and Satan are applicable to you. In the next chapter we will develop the implications of this objective truth as we talk about what it means to walk in newness of life. Jesus makes it possible for you to experience, by faith in His grace operating in you, a true life-change.

5
WHERE DO WE GET
THE POWER TO MORPH?

EPHESIANS 4:7–10

I 'm glad you stayed with me as we worked through so much background material. It is pivotal that we understand what the work of Christ actually accomplished. Though foreign to our ears, the lights would have definitely come on in the minds of Paul's first-century audience when they heard the rich language he used. Paul's announcement meant that the siege of sin had been broken and the penalty of sin would no longer hang over our heads. The archenemy Satan had been defeated. Finally, the glorious Messiah had invaded the "lower parts of the earth" and proclaimed His victory in fulfillment of hundreds of years of prophecy.

Imagine the excitement and liberation that those early Christians experienced as they read Paul's words for the first time. They didn't just cheer because someone explained what Paul meant; they cheered because they understood the vast scope and spiritual power in the message. Paul's announcement had the effect of a lightning bolt! They felt the shock of God's power to transform their lives.

Unfortunately, in our day this amazing work of Christ and the journey between the Cross and the Resurrection has been reduced to something we casually call the Easter Story. For many of us, the events at the end of Christ's earthly ministry have been oversimplified. And for most of us, our Easter experience has become superficial.

I don't know about you, but for most of my early life, Easter and the gospel message were somehow lost in the mechanics of buying a new set of clothes, watching my mother put Easter lilies on display, going half asleep at a sunrise service, mumbling through the song "Christ the Lord Is Risen Today," and hurrying home for an Easter egg hunt.

Later, even as a new believer, the Easter message was still limited to the bare minimum (Christ came; He died for my sin; He rose from the dead; He paid for our sin. Receive Jesus as your Savior and He'll forgive your sins, too.) I don't say this tritely, nor do I think we can or should attempt to change that story in any way. Those facts do make up the core of the gospel message. But in order to fully comprehend the gospel message, we must move beyond the summary and learn the depth and implications of all that God has done on our behalf. The apostle Paul wanted his first readers to know that profound events occurred between Christ's death and resurrection that directly impacted the possibility of radical life-change.

In our day, many do not understand or know how to apply the truth that Paul taught. We come close to fitting Paul's sobering description, "having a form of godliness but denying its power" (2 Timothy 3:5). We desperately need to experience the fullness of God and affirm as well as experience all His power to transform us.

Instead, the average professing believer in America who says he trusts in Christ may be able to add, "I know He died on the cross and rose from the grave." He may also say, "I committed my life to Christ at a camp or a church and invited Him to be my Savior—to come into my heart." But those "believers" frequently don't give any observable evidence that belief in Jesus has made any difference in the way they actually live. Belief in Jesus doesn't make a big difference in where they spend their time, how they handle their sexuality, how they keep their priorities, how they do marriage, or how they parent. It seems to make little or no impact in the areas of personal integrity or work ethic. Do you know why? Because we may know the story of Easter, but we just don't get it. Oh, we may get the part about the free gift of salvation, and of course we want that, but we don't get the foundational truths about what was accomplished at the Cross and before the Resurrection. That is the core, the basis for life-change—holy transformation.

Actually, I think a lot of people just don't know because they haven't been taught. The unfortunate truth is that we have developed a culture among evangelical believers in which no one is surprised when a person prays to receive Christ yet very little change occurs in that person's life. My heart goes out continually to people who find themselves stuck in a dilemma. *Christ lives in me,* they think, *but I'm still sinning a lot. I'm still struggling with the same stuff. What's wrong with me? Is there something wrong with the gospel?* They don't know how life-change occurs. Somewhere along the line they didn't connect with other believers. They didn't get into the Bible. And they didn't learn the principles of spiritual growth. After a while they began to say, *Well, I know I'm a Christian, I guess. I don't know how it works. It sure is hard. Boy, I hope I go to heaven.* Maybe this sequence if painfully familiar to you because you have lived it. Little by little you just digressed to the same previous way of life. Today you're back to that old vague hunger for change.

This doesn't have to be your spiritual biography! The apostle Paul explained some profound theological truths that apply to your life. Understanding them will create the foundation for genuine change and for your personal transformation. For the remainder of this chapter I want to develop the three core principles for life-change found in Ephesians 4:7–10.

But to each one of us grace has been given as Christ apportioned it. This is why it says:

> "When he ascended on high,
> he led captives in his train
> and gave gifts to men."

(What does "he ascended" mean except that he also descended to the lower, earthly regions? He who descended is the very one who ascended higher than all the heavens, in order to fill the whole universe.)

THE FIRST PRINCIPLE OF TRANSFORMATION: LIFE-CHANGE ALWAYS BEGINS WITH THE TRUTH

The first principle of transformation is this: *Life-change always begins with the truth.* Life-change—morphing—doesn't begin with an experience. It's always rooted in the truth. The last night Jesus was on the earth He prayed, "[Father], make them pure and holy" (John 17:17a NLT). How? "By teaching them your words of truth" (v. 17b NLT). He basically said, "God, I want them to reflect who We are and what We're like." And then he stated how that happens—by truth. Where do we get the truth? We get truth from God's Word.

A group of Jews believed in Jesus early in his ministry. In John 8:31–32, He told them, "If you abide in My word [*abide* means to take it in and act on it], you are My disciples indeed. And you shall know the truth, and the truth shall make you free" (NKJV). You can be free. How many Christians do you know who are free? Are they really free of the same old habits they struggled with? Free of anger outbursts, free of lust, free to really live in a loving, authentic way? Jesus promised that such change is possible. He gave His word to them, and He gives the same word to you and me.

So where do we find freeing truth in this passage from Ephesians? These verses describe Christ as the conquering victor over sin, death, and Satan. You and I need to respond more deeply to that claim than just nodding our heads. Christ's victory happened at the Cross, and the Resurrection proved it. When He went into Hades and to paradise, He stormed those places as a conquering victor. The reason we have gifts is because those are the spoils of His victory. The power to live a new life was made possible by His death and resurrection. The power isn't about trying hard or "doing good." Philippians 2:13 says, "For God is working in you, giving you the desire to obey him and the power to do what pleases him" (NLT). Christianity isn't about moralistic efforts. It's not a code of ethics. It's about a relationship. But here's the fact: That relationship is rooted in truth.

The truth underlying our relationship with Christ is this: The power of sin has been broken. You don't have to sin. You don't have to be addicted to alcohol. You don't have to be addicted to pleasing people. That power has been broken. Not only the power of sin, but the power and penalty of death. You don't have to be afraid. Paul asked the question in 1 Corinthians 15:55, "Death, where is your sting?" (NLT). He knew the answer. Death's sting had been removed by Christ's victory. It's been swallowed up by Christ's resurrection. So sin is a defeated foe in your life. Your fear of the future and death is defeated in your life, and Satan is defeated. *The only power it now has is the power you give it.* Read that sentence again, slowly. That means that the only power Satan, sin, and death have over you comes from what you give them.

You don't have to be deceived by the world's system any more. You don't have to watch the TV tube and be duped by the advertisements telling you to look a certain way or have certain things or be this or be that in order to be fulfilled. Our culture tells us lies, and we believe them enough to invest time and money. When the promises don't work, we get depressed so we get drugs for our depression. Eventually, we realize that those who are telling us what will make us happy are wrong. You don't have to be deceived. Colossians 2 tells us that when Jesus died on the cross, He disarmed, displayed, and destroyed the works of the great deceiver (see Colossians 2:13–15). Greater is He that is in us as believers than he that is in the world (see 1 John 4:4). As you can see, until you come to grasp the objective truth about what Christ has accomplished for you there's no hope for change! **Genuine life-change always begins with the truth.**

A Personal Example

Let me picture how this plays out in a person's life. My dad didn't grow up as a Christian. He's a great guy. The most telling characteristics of his life for a long time had to do with his experiences as an ex-Marine. He grew up during the Depression. When he was thirteen, his father died. By the time he was fifteen, the family farm had been sold out from under him. He and my grandmother had to go live with an older married sister. When he was a little over sixteen he lied about his age and/or got his mother to sign a waiver so he could enlist to fight in World War II. He saw action on Guam, Iwo Jima, and other South Pacific battlefields. Can you imagine being a seventeen-year-old 50-caliber machine-gunner?

He rarely talks about the war, but on a few occasions he has shared glimpses of the horror of killing hundreds and hundreds of enemy soldiers as a teenager. He witnessed the carnage of hand-to-hand combat and the horror of suicide attacks. By the time his war years were over, he had accumulated a lifetime's worth of scenes for nightmares. Along the way, he learned what every good Marine learns: how to smoke three packs of cigarettes a day, how to drink more beer than the average guy, and how to bust you right in the nose if you messed with him.

In spite of all that, Dad turned out to be a committed father, a tough cookie who loved me a lot. I've learned to appreciate what he has had to overcome in life. His early experiences were handled by the wisdom of his generation. Men weren't expected to be sensitive. No one asked, "Do you have any lingering traumatic issues in your life that you got from the war? Have you ever heard of delayed stress syndrome? Would you like to talk about your feelings? Are you hurting deep inside?" Instead, he stuffed it all. Over the years, those unresolved issues began to raise their ugly heads in Dad's life. He gradually drank more and more to escape what he couldn't face. As we kids got older and as he and my mom worked through the normal midlife issues, there got to be some real tension in our home. Dad was always good to us, never violent, but he became increasingly absent.

Eventually I went away to college. One by one, my family members became Christians. Campus Crusade led my sister to Christ, and her life was so different that I asked, "What do you have?" The Fellowship of Christian Athletes introduced me to Christ. Then I met a bricklayer trained by the Navigators who taught me the basics, because I knew nothing about the Christian life. All I knew was I had a new life, amazing peace, and a sudden interest in the Bible. I had never checked the Bible out, even though I went to church growing up. But after coming to Christ I read the Bible voraciously, and God began to change my desires. No one ever came to me and said, "Stop doing this, and stop doing that," or "You gotta do this, and you gotta do that" to be a good Christian. I just began to read the Bible in the morning and the night and was around a group of loving people who were authentic and living it out. I watched God change them. I experienced God changing me.

Home Again

I came home after my freshman year to discover that God was at work in the rest of my family. Dad seemed restless. He shocked me one day by asking, "Chip, what's happened to you?"

I answered, "What do you mean?"

He said, "You're different."

I sheepishly confessed, "Well, Dad, I asked Christ to come into my life about a year ago." Until that time I was reluctant to tell my parents. After trusting Christ, I hid my Bible under my pillow for the first six months and read it every morning and every night. It was all so new to me. I assumed they wouldn't understand.

To my everlasting astonishment, my father followed up my admission of faith in Christ with a question, "Son, what have you got? Whatever you have, I think I need it."

My ignorance kicked in one second behind my surprise. I didn't know what to say or where to start. I had never tried to put my faith into words for someone else. Now I think I would say, "Oh, Dad, the problem was my sin. Christ died on the cross to pay for my sin and yours. He's your substitute like He is mine. What you need to do is be honest with yourself, accept that you have sinned, come to Him repentantly, and ask Him to forgive you. He'll come into your life, forgive your sins, and you'll begin the transformation process." Unfortunately, none of that came to mind. Instead, I said, "Dad, all I know is that I started reading the Bible, and I prayed a prayer, and then a lot of things started changing inside of me." How's that for a brilliant presentation of the gospel?

So my Dad started on the truth. As a good Marine, he did it the right way. He got up at 5:30 every morning and read the Bible for an hour. Three months passed. My father repeatedly read through the Gospels: Matthew, Mark, Luke, John; Matthew, Mark, Luke, John. About the third time through the

Gospels he commented, "You know, a lot of these stories sound similar. Is there something wrong with me?" He didn't know that he was reading four biographies of Jesus. He just didn't get it—yet. But he kept at it. He kept looking into the truth of God's Word. **Life-change always begins with the truth.** It's not just an experience, it's not an activity, it's not just an event, it's not coming to church, it's not trying to be a good person, it's not throwing up a few prayers —it's always rooted in truth.

The Truth

Now, before I finish telling you about my father's quest for holy transformation, I want to remind you of the central point of this story. Here's the point we are highlighting at this moment. Immediately after Jesus died on the cross and paid for your sin, He invaded the stronghold of evil and conquered sin, death, and Satan. That means you are free, you are forgiven, and you are secure. Sin has been utterly defeated, including your own sin. That's the truth. But it doesn't end there. Christ's victory is a fact. His victory is our starting point. Life-change begins with truth. But simply knowing the truth is never enough!

THE SECOND PRINCIPLE OF TRANSFORMATION:
LIFE-CHANGE DEMANDS THAT WE ACT ON THE TRUTH

The second principle follows the first one closely: *Life-change demands that we act on the truth.* That kind of action goes by the title "faith." Life-change demands that we act on the truth. Notice what Paul's picture of Christ's action in the grave implies. We become co-partakers of Christ's victory over sin, death, and Satan. We join the winning side. When? The moment we receive Christ as our personal savior by faith. He broke the power of sin. He destroyed death. He destroyed the works of the devil. That is a true, objective, historic reality. But we don't get in on it until by faith we say, "I believe. Lord Jesus, come into my life." The moment that happens, our past is put behind us, the Spirit of God comes in, our sins are forgiven, and we are "in Christ." Now, as newborn spiritual babies, we immediately begin the process of holy transformation (sanctification), as little by little God takes the old away and transforms us into the likeness of His Son. God will morph us; He will change us. That's the picture. But it's not enough simply to know the truth. That's the basis. The second thing we have to do is to act on faith. Now, back to Dad's story.

A Personal Example—Continued

Dad faithfully read the Gospels for three months. He said, "Hey, I don't really get it. I'm still outside, looking in. How do I get in?"

I said, "I don't know, Dad." Frankly, I hadn't learned much more in the three months since he began his journey. I added, "All I know is, keep reading."

I could see the longing and spiritual hunger in his eyes. There was so much he couldn't put into words. He simply nodded and said, "OK."

Three more months passed. He continued his steady Gospel diet along with expanded sections of the New Testament. Finally he said, "I still don't know what it's all about, but there's one thing I know for sure."

I asked, "What's that, Dad?" He had just spent six months living with Jesus and the disciples. I really wanted to know what he had found.

"Somewhere at the heart of this whole deal is faith," he began. "I mean, it just keeps coming up. However you get in, however this relationship with God works, at the core is faith."

After six months of exposure to God's truth, my Dad was hitting upon the central theme of the New Testament—faith. His discovery would soon transform him from a religious, church-going unbeliever to a child of God. What an insight. I know a lot of Christians who have been believers for five or ten years who still don't get that. They think the Christian life is primarily about morality—you have to do more good deeds than bad deeds. Or it's an ethical code to live by. "I want to act Christianly," they mumble. Or "I should treat people this way or that way." Instead of being free and alive and transformed from the inside out, they struggle with piles of "oughts," "shoulds," rules, and guilt. They try to "clean up the outside of the cup" (see Matthew 23:25) while their private lives don't match their claims. The Christian life becomes one of duty rather than delight. They live under a load of man-made religion rather than the freedom of a God-ordained relationship.

Do you want to know what God really wants

from you more than anything else in the world? That you believe on Him whom the Father sent (see John 17). That's what my Dad discovered firsthand in the Gospels. That truth became the turning point in his life when he acted on it. Dad shared with me later that one day during this time of searching he walked by his dresser and saw a "Four Spiritual Laws" booklet lying on top of it. Prompted by God, he sat on the bed and read through it. As he read that simple outline of the gospel, the lights came on. He realized exactly what it meant to have faith. It meant that he needed to believe and place his trust in what Christ had done for him on the cross and in His resurrection. Without a lot of fanfare, my dad closed the bedroom door, got down on his knees next to the bed, and prayed the prayer printed in the back of that booklet. He admitted to God that he had sinned, and he realized that even all the horror he had been through in the war could be forgiven by a loving God because of Christ's work on the cross. He accepted God's free gift of salvation through Jesus and asked Him to come into his life. My Dad spent six months searching for the truth. But what ignited his transformation was that he acted on the truth that he received.

The Question

So let me ask you, Do you believe? Not, Do you go to church? Not, Are you moral? Not, Do you give to the United Way? Not, Do you send up a prayer now and then? Not, Are you trying hard? There are millions of people naming the name of Christ all over

America who do those things. But I'm telling you, on the authority of God's Word, that those things don't give you a relationship with the living God.

The problem with Christianity is it has turned into a religion. God never intended it to be a religion. He intended it to be a breakthrough into a personal relationship with Him. A breakthrough to remove the barrier of sin between Him and us forever. A breakthrough in which the Father and we could have intimacy and love and forgiveness and peace and joy and power over sin. A breakthrough that would allow us to face death and look it square in the eye and say, "I'm not afraid to die. Not because I'm a good person, but because I have received by faith the work of Christ."

So, how about you? Have you acted on the truth that God has given you? You may know the story of Jesus and His love for you, but have you personally asked Him to be your Savior and Lord? **If not, let me encourage you to act on the truth you know right now!**

THE THIRD PRINCIPLE OF TRANSFORMATION: LIFE-CHANGE IS BOTH A GIFT AND A RESPONSIBILITY

By now you may begin to see why so many people know about Christ and even intellectually believe in Him but have experienced very little genuine life-change. As we've seen, life-change always begins with the truth. What many people don't understand is what we've learned here. But there's more. In Ephesians 4:7–10, we'll learn there is a third and vital principle for holy transformation: *Life-change is both a gift and a responsibility.* Let me repeat that: Life-change is both a gift and a responsibility. Holy transformation is something only God can accomplish in us. But that does not mean that we are passive. No one can change on his or her own. Only God can change a life, but God chooses never to do this alone. There are specific responsibilities for each of us in the life-change process.

Farmers have many illustrations of this truth. You can put seed in the ground but you can't make it grow. But you can choose an environment where there's sunshine and fertilizer. Spiritual growth follows the same pattern. Only God can bring about growth, but you can do all that you can to produce the right kind of conditions.

Paul used this very parallel to explain spiritual transformation to the Corinthian church. "My job was to plant the seed in your hearts, and Apollos watered it, but it was God, not we, who made it grow. The ones who do the planting or watering aren't important, but God is important because he is the one who makes the seed grow" (1 Corinthians 3:6–7 NLT). Only God can change you. Sure, you can clean some things up and you can work hard and you can listen to tapes on the way to work and talk to yourself about being a good person. You can discipline your life and you can make some progress. But your growth will be limited to your human efforts. That's not the kind of growth I'm talking about here.

I'm talking about growth from the inside out. I'm talking about the transformation of the secret thoughts. I'm talking about such a change in your capacity to love that your reactions are loving toward someone who's hurt you. It's supernatural. I'm talking about facing strong, long-standing addictions and experiencing the power of God to help you understand "I am free," seeing Him work and move in your life. I'm talking about saying by faith, "The Bible says God really loves me; I'm going to believe that to the point of taking a step of faith." As you take that step, the grace of God floods you and you start to become a dad like your kids have never seen or a mom like they never dreamed they could have. Or you begin to treat your mate in an unconditional way instead of demanding certain changes on her or his part before you will do your part. You stop saying, "When she gets a little more affectionate, then this marriage will really get going," or "If he becomes more sensitive, then maybe we'll have a better home life." Instead you say, "By the grace of God I'm going to give her what God would give her. I'm going to love her, I'm going to love him unconditionally even if I get nothing back." You do that with supernatural power. And then you see radical change, holy transformation. It is something only the Spirit of God can accomplish in the heart of a believer by His grace. Genuine spiritual transformation is a work of God— a work of grace. It is a gift.

The Gift of Grace

It's important, however, when we think about God's grace, that we don't equate grace with passivity.

Grace means God's unmerited favor, a gift from Him. But how God gets grace to us is a whole other story. He doesn't simply get grace to us in a vacuum. God gives grace not only through His Spirit and His Word but also through the lives of other people. That's why we said that holy transformation is not only a gift but also a responsibility. What Paul is going to teach, beginning at Ephesians 4:7, is that God has supernaturally endowed every single believer with a spiritual gift, given by His grace, that is to be used, empowered by His Spirit, to help other believers morph. That means that you and I, at the moment we received Christ, also received from God a supernatural ability that allows us to give to other people the grace of God. What an amazing way that God had chosen to let us participate in the process of holy transformation. Ephesians 4:7 says, "But to each one of us grace was given" (NASB). Each one—every single believer—receives a gift. If you know Christ, if you've received Him, if your sins are forgiven and the Spirit of God dwells in you, the moment you came to Christ you got an endowment.

This particular *gift of grace* is a different term from *spiritual gift.* This is a word for a sacred trust. It's a sacred trust for the purpose of service. The grace gift has to do with the *capacity* for service; the spiritual gift part has to do with the *area* of service. Not only does every believer have one, but the verse adds, "According to the measure of Christ's gift" (v. 7 NASB). That little phrase means it's given exactly to fit who you are so that your life and purpose will achieve God's highest glory and will bring about the greatest joy in your life. Both God's grace and God's gift are tailor-made for you.

You have a spiritual ability the moment you come to Christ to serve and love and empower other people. **Only God can bring about change, but He never chooses to do it alone.** I don't know why. He chooses to have us as the church live in community together and love one another and operate out of our giftedness in a way that transformation occurs. When we live in authentic community, we act as catalysts for morphing in each other's lives. There are at least two reasons why holy transformation occurs in the context of meaningful community relationships. The first reason for community is to remind us that life-change occurs on the basis of grace, not self-effort. We're not "on our own." Life-change, transformation, metamorphosis, God in you—the spiritual gift reminds you every time you use it that this isn't about trying hard. This isn't about earning God's favor—it's *grace.*

The second reason behind Christ's gift in community is to empower us as other-centered agents of grace who supply what others need to become like Christ. Life-change never happens in isolation. God wants to change you. The tools and resources He uses are the spiritual gifts of *other* people as you live in humility and love and genuine relationship *together.* It is their spiritual gifts and Christ in them that God uses along with the truth of His Word, empowered by the Spirit to bring about supernatural transformation.

The above two reasons explain why holy transformation is only occurring in the lives of some 10 percent of the Christians in America. Think it through

for yourself. The apostle Paul has clearly taught us
that transformation always begins with the truth.
That means that life-change will demand that people
take very seriously getting into the truth. Most believers in America do not have a steady diet of God's
Word. We've also learned that simply knowing the
truth will not bring about transformation. It requires
that we act on it by faith. Even a casual glance at the
average believer reveals that people are not putting
into practice on a daily basis what they are learning
in God's Word. And, finally, we have learned that
God's grace is received not only from His Word and
by His Spirit, but by the full participation of His
people as they discover and use their gifts in authentic community. When people understand their
gifts and are connected with other believers in a
meaningful way, God uses that very environment to
carry out His powerful morphing work.

The Picture Today

By contrast, Christianity in America is far too often characterized by people who come to church
now and then, sit down, listen to a sermon, nod a little bit, intellectually assimilate it to some level, and
then leave and live the same way the world lives.
Passive faith leads to little transformation. Active
participation in the body of Christ makes transformation unavoidable. So many Christians are missing
out. It breaks my heart! It breaks God's heart! It nul-
lifies and devalues the great sacrificial work of Christ
for each one of us. Now we are coming to grips with

why so many believers' lives simply aren't changing. Instead of understanding our position in Christ and the objective truth of what's been accomplished for us, we have been seduced by the world into believing that satisfaction will come with:

- a little more money
- a little better job
- a successful family with kids who are upwardly mobile, good students, and sports stars

or

- when I get some nicer clothes
- when we get the second house
- when we get a better car
- when we remodel the kitchen
- when we can finally afford better vacations and a hot tub in the backyard.

I don't say that harshly, nor do I mean in any way that having nice things, when priorities are in order, are bad at all. I'm talking about assumptions by millions of Christians who are settling for the emptiness of this world's pursuits instead of embarking on the exciting adventure of "seeking God's kingdom and His righteousness," knowing that everything else will fall into place (see Matthew 6:33).

You and I will only experience the morphing supernatural power of the living God when we understand the power God unleashed between the time

Christ died and was resurrected. He utterly defeated sin, death, and Satan.

CONCLUSION

Perhaps you realize that the truth facing you right now is that maybe you have never really believed in Christ. You have never asked Him to apply His transforming power to your life. If so, I invite you to act by faith today. If you have never received Christ, say, "Lord Jesus, I want in. I want to receive the free gift. I turn, I repent from my old way of thinking, and I ask you to come into my life." If you do that, you will have given God permission to begin morphing you. Whether you are a new believer or a present believer, I also urge you to carefully ponder what kind of person you really want to be and then consider praying the following prayer:

"Holy Father, I'm going to get into Your Word regularly and get connected to a Bible-teaching church at a deep level. I'm going to discover my spiritual gift and practice it. Today is my last day in passive Christianity—I'm going to live by faith, trusting You to transform me into someone who looks and acts a lot like Jesus."

You do that for the next six months, and I can guarantee you will not be disappointed. You will be changed. God loves to do amazing things with ordinary lives. You can hardly imagine what He can do with yours. Now, if you are wondering how this works, if you want to know where to start and how to get yourself in a position where you could actually begin to experience God's grace, well, that's what the next chapter is all about.

6
A LOOK AT ONE
TRANSFORMED LIFE

EPHESIANS 4:11–16

U p to this point we have discussed at length the truth, the necessity, and the basis of holy transformation. Now it's time to look at the specifics of God's game plan. The last few chapters have focused on your role and opportunity as a full member of God's team, the church. Now it's time to start seeing how the team functions together, using all the individual parts, under the guidance and control of the coach and master, Jesus Christ.

In order for you to grasp how dramatically God can and does change lives today, I'd like to begin this chapter with an e-mail I received from someone reporting on his life before and after he began to understand how holy transformation works. I've received permission to share this account and have changed the names to protect privacy.

This account comes from the trenches. The marriage and family you are about to meet are of regular,

average, American Christians attending a solid, evangelical church. This story represents what happens
when a typical man suddenly gets very honest with
his real condition before God and with his family. Not
only does he begin to see himself, he also begins to
understand the process we've been talking about in
these chapters. Following the e-mail, I'd like to give
you an overview of God's game plan for how you, like
this man and his family, can begin to evaluate where
you are spiritually and take necessary steps toward
holy transformation.

Now I'll let Joe tell you the details of his story.

Dear Chip,

I don't know where to begin, or how to thank
Santa Cruz Bible Church and you. You see, I wrote
you a while back explaining that my marriage was
in deep trouble. I asked if the church provided any
type of counseling. You e-mailed me back and got
us connected with the reconciliation program,
which we entered three months ago.

One of my first big discoveries was that my
priorities were completely out of whack. God
didn't even appear in my list of top forty. Now
He's #1! I had been neglecting everything that
was important to me (to us) for a very long time.
We appeared like a perfect couple to others, but
we were actually completely disconnected from
God and from each other.

Bottom line, I was a jerk. I wasn't abusive in
any way, but just not there for my family. Highlights from a minor league hockey team on TV,

my hobbies, or just being a grouch were much more important to me than talking with my wife, taking time with our daughter, or spending any time, let alone quality time, with the family.

Our house was falling apart, literally. Leaks in the plumbing had gone unattended for almost two years. Meanwhile, figurative leaks in communication and caring had been draining our marriage for a lot longer.

I hope you get the picture. I was not mean, lazy, or an abusive father. I had no drug or alcohol problems. Probably like men in many homes, I kept telling myself that everything was just fine. Deep down, I knew I was lying.

I wrote my first letter as a result of a confrontation with my wife. She sent a loud and clear signal that if something did not change, she would . . . I think you can guess the outcome that was looming in our future. We were on the verge of becoming another divorce statistic. I turned to the church with few expectations and with few hopes that anything could really be done for our situation. The prospect of actually losing my family finally got my attention.

Our progress in the last three months can be summarized by one word—Wow! Our first service back in church [life-change begins with the truth] after a long time of sporadic attendance was the Sunday after Father's Day. You seemed to be preaching your message about responsible and godly fatherhood right at me. The illustrations seemed to be lifted out of my previous week. You presented some very specific action steps from the Scriptures. I'll never forget how you ended the message—"Men, get off your rear ends and do this for your family!" You might just as well have added, "And Joe, I'm talking to you in particular."

I knew I couldn't walk away from that challenge. But I also realized in that crystal-clear moment that the most messed-up relationship in my life was my relationship with God. I knew I was so far out of touch with what God wanted in my life that I couldn't expect my family to take seriously anything I said or did. I needed supernatural help!

One of the opportunities offered that Sunday was a class to prepare for baptism. I signed up. My wife raised an eyebrow. I had just done something totally out of character for me. She didn't say a thing, but she was watching. I'm sure she guessed that if the class conflicted with my favorite TV show, I would miss the baptism instruction. I didn't miss the class, but I quickly discovered that baptism wasn't about doing something religious and saving my marriage—it was about declaring a relationship with Jesus I wasn't that sure I had. Once I confessed my sins and accepted Him as Lord and Savior [life-change demands we act on the truth], it seemed like one of the most natural things in the world to walk into the water with all my clothes on, get tipped over backward, and come up feeling like I couldn't wait for God to ask me to do something else—no matter how difficult. That turned out to be God helping me [transformation is rooted in grace] make caring for my wife and kids the most important immediate job I could do out of gratitude for God's forgiveness.

My wife and I have almost completed our reconciliation program. God's reshaping of my life, and the guidance we've gotten has brought about miraculous changes [supernatural life-change is God's norm for all of us] in our marriage and in our home. My wife gave her enthusiastic OK to this list:

- We are once again deeply in love with each other, more than we have ever been.
- We are both reading the Scriptures daily.
- We have become members of the church, eager to find ways to participate.
- We went to our first small group meeting last Sunday, and we're excited to find other couples working through the same struggles we are and finding that God offers all kinds of help!
- Our twelve-year-old daughter came to Christ this year at church camp.
- The plumbing in our house got fixed, along with other odd jobs I had been neglecting.
- One of the men's groups has invited me to join, and I can hardly wait.

- I am taking my younger son with me to Promise Keepers next week.

- We have our car and home radio tuned to the station that carries *Living on the Edge*.

- Our whole family is exploring Christian music and finding all kinds of favorites.

- I've been listening to Bible-teaching tapes on my drive to work and I find myself reflecting on the truth of God's Word all day.

- Our twenty-year-old son has begun to read the daily devotional material while he serves in the military overseas. In almost every e-mail he sends home, he writes, "I'm just amazed at what's happening to you, Mom and Dad!"

Everything is different. My life has gone through a huge transformation.

Basically, our lives together have been drastically changed in ways I never thought possible. Frankly, if someone had told me four months ago that even one of the items in the list above was possible, I would have said, "No way." Now I know that "God makes ways where there seems to be no way." I know there will be bumps ahead, and I don't at all expect life to be easy. But walking with God sure beats trying to live on my own. I know that God is there for us and we can turn to Him at anytime, for anything. The future is now brighter than it ever has been!

Thanks for your part!

Joe

What thoughts and feelings went through you as you read that e-mail? Did it touch on some of the issues in your life? Did you notice that many of the lessons we have already learned together were put into practice or experienced by this man and his family? Did you notice the emphasis on truth, on God's Word, on community, on applying God's Word? And how God over the weeks and months began the transformation process? To what degree have you experienced God working the same way in your life? In what areas would you like to see God work in your life or family in the future?

As you think about where you sense change needs to occur in your life, I want to help you take the next steps in learning and participating in God's game plan for your holy transformation. As we continue our journey through Ephesians 4, you will learn what God has in mind for you and every single believer who is willing to do life His way.

EPHESIANS 4:11-16

Follow along as we walk through Ephesians 4:11–16 (using the NASB text). It begins with a gift described in Ephesians 4:11:

> He gave some as apostles, and some as prophets, and some as evangelists, and some as pastors and teachers.

God gives a group of gifted leaders to the church for a purpose. Why? The next verse explains:

> For the equipping of the saints for the work of
> service, to the building up of the body of Christ.

God provides leaders to help believers involved in practical ministry to develop and apply their gifts in such a way that synergy occurs, empowered by the Holy Spirit. What does the building up of the body look like? What's the goal? Look at verse 13.

> Until we all [every believer—not some, not a few, not the superstars, not missionaries, not pastors] attain to the unity of the faith and of the knowledge of the Son of God, to a mature man, to the measure of the stature which belongs to the fullness of Christ.

In other words, gifted leaders equip (prepare) all of us ordinary, regular Christians to use our gifts so that every single person in the body of Christ becomes mature. So that each one becomes like Christ. So that you and I reach our full potential spiritually. The efforts of gifted leaders equipping the saints for the work of ministry have a vivid result. You become like Jesus. You begin to think like Jesus. You begin to act like Jesus. You begin to love like Jesus. And you begin to respond to your enemies like Jesus because He's doing supernatural work in your life.

Now, lest that get kind of foggy, sentimental, and purely theoretical, the next three verses provide a clear-cut description of spiritual maturity—what it really looks like to be like Jesus. Verses 14 through 16 give us four evidences of spiritual maturity (again, using the NASB text). These four measurable results will characterize your life as you become spiritually mature, or transformed into the likeness of Christ (vv. 14–15).

> As a result, we are no longer to be children, tossed here and there by waves and carried about by every wind of doctrine, by the trickery of men, by craftiness in deceitful scheming; but [in contrast] speaking the truth in love, we are to grow up in all aspects into Him who is the head, even Christ.

How does that kind of maturity develop? Christ Himself is the power behind the scenes (v. 16):

> From whom the whole body, being fitted and held together by what every joint supplies, according to the proper working of each individual part, causes the growth of the body for the building up of itself in love.

FOUR TESTS OF SPIRITUAL MATURITY

We'll look at them in detail a little later, but this text provides the following four tests of your spiritual maturity:

1. You can handle the Scriptures well enough to spot false teachers and trendy religious fads. You can maintain doctrinal stability in the face of either one.

2. You have the ability to speak the truth in love. Your commitment to relationships allows you to say the hard things, but you say them in a loving way.

3. You are fitted. You are participating fully, you know your gift, you're a part of the body, you're functioning in your gift and fruit is being produced through you because you fit a niche in the body that only you can fill.

4. And finally, the ultimate evidence of spiritual maturity is an ever-expanding love for God and others. The acid test when someone asks, "How are you doing in your spiritual life?" is not what activities you're doing or not doing. I believe God measures our spiritual progress by the way we answer the following two questions:

   • Am I loving God more deeply?
   • Am I loving others more authentically?

When we're doing that, we are progressing in spiritual maturity.

DESIGNED FOR SPIRITUAL GROWTH

Those six verses we just surveyed include four timeless "keys" about how God can make you the person you long to be. Those keys outline God's plan to create an environment in which people grow. If we are part of a local church that practices the four truths that flow out of this passage, we will find that authentic transformation will actually occur in the lives of ordinary people like the man who wrote that e-mail we read, or his wife, or you, or me.

So, let's get practical. How does the process of holy transformation really work? How can what happened in Joe's life happen in yours? Join me in the next chapter as we take a closer look at the grace-filled environment God has designed to encourage your growth to maturity.

7
LET'S GET PRACTICAL!
OR GOD'S GAME PLAN

EPHESIANS 4:11–16

I f you are anything like me, the story you read in the last chapter about Joe and his family represents the kind of dynamic changes that you want to see happen in your life. No matter how far along you are in the spiritual life or how recently you have become a believer, a personal report like Joe's serves as a powerful motivation toward desiring all the positive growth God has planned for you and for me.

Now it's time to get down to "brass tacks." How does the process actually work? You know what Christ has done; now what do you need to do? What's God's game plan? How can you put into practice what you just learned about His divinely designed organism called the church so that you can receive grace that will transform you from the inside out? If you really long to see God change your life, take a deep breath, roll up your mental sleeves, and take a closer look at Ephesians 4:11–16 (using the

NIV), where God provides for us His practical game plan for holy transformation. As you read through the text, pay close attention to the sequence of keys that outline the ways and means God will use to morph you into the likeness of Christ.

> It was he who gave some to be apostles, some to be prophets, some to be evangelists, and some to be pastors and teachers, to prepare God's people for works of service, so that the body of Christ may be built up until we all reach unity in the faith and in the knowledge of the Son of God and become mature, attaining to the whole measure of the fullness of Christ.
>
> Then we will no longer be infants, tossed back and forth by the waves, and blown here and there by every wind of teaching and by the cunning and craftiness of men in their deceitful scheming. Instead, speaking the truth in love, we will in all things grow up into him who is the Head, that is, Christ. From him the whole body, joined and held together by every supporting ligament, grows and builds itself up in love, as each part does its work.

At first glance, you may ask, "What does this passage have to do with God changing my life? It talks about prophets, evangelists, and apostles. What parts of this passage can really help change me from the inside out?" Follow along carefully, because those six verses contain the details of God's divine design for the church, of which you became a part the moment you received Christ. If you do not understand how God meant for His church to function, you will never be able to tap into the grace that is available there. How you fulfill your role in the church is at the heart of allowing God to bring about the life-change you desperately desire and which He has promised to provide. Let's take a brief look at these leaders given to us by God to help us grow.

Key 1
Leaders Are Gifted to Equip God's People for Service

Notice the opening words of the passage: "And He gave." That phrase is really important. Several Bible translations capitalize the pronoun so there's no confusion about the source of the gifts. Transformation begins with grace and it ends with grace. God gives significant leaders in different places to help mature His body. But the focus is never to be on the leader. The focus is always to be on the One who gives the leader or the leaders. God doesn't want you to think your Bible study leader is the most wonderful person in the world and you couldn't live without him. He's a gift from God; she's a gift from God. God doesn't want you to place any spiritual leader in a position only He Himself can occupy. In the process of transformation, the focus has to be on the author of transformation. God gives gifts, even the gifts that are people.

Apostles

Paul places *apostles* at the head of the list of the people-gifts God gives. Originally the term simply referred to someone who was given a divine commission. The Bible calls quite a few people apostles. Jesus called and commissioned twelve apostles for very unusual service. After Judas's suicide, the eleven disciples chose Mathias to replace him. Later, James (Jesus' brother) is called an apostle. Paul also became an apostle. Eventually, the term came to refer, in the New Testament, to those who were eyewitnesses to the risen Christ and had received a divine commission.

In our day there are no more apostles in this strict New Testament sense of the word. Today however, many people use this word to describe leaders that are pioneers and church planters. This usage takes us back to the original meaning of the word, which simply designated a messenger. The primary apostolic gift God has given was fulfilled by those eyewitnesses of the Resurrection who carried out their commission and provided the very foundation for the New Testament church through their writings. The apostles continue to speak their message to the church as we give careful attention to the New Testament. Those who start new works and lead us in upholding, studying, and applying God's message are fulfilling a secondary apostolic role today.

Prophets

The second group on Paul's list are *prophets*. We tend to think of prophets as either the fire-breathing preachers of the Old Testament or the wild predictors of the supermarket tabloid headlines. The original prophets gave exact warnings about the future and revealed truth from God. Today's "prophets" seem more driven by the desire for notoriety and profits than by any interest in telling the truth to warn and guide people. Actually, the biblical gift of prophecy is not nearly as concerned with foretelling as it is with "forth-telling." Prophets were the people in the early church who communicated God's Word with such power that life-change occurred within the people who heard their message.

Throughout biblical history until the close of the New Testament, God gave direct revelation to the prophets. That revelation became the New Testament documents. Ephesians 2:20 tells us that the church has been "built on the foundation of the apostles and prophets, Christ Jesus Himself being the corner stone" (NASB). Strictly speaking, the gift of prophecy, with an emphasis on foretelling the future or giving new revelation from God, is not operating in our day. It was a foundational gift. However, the prophetic ministry of forth-telling and proclaiming God's Word continues as the church is built upon the truth given to us through Jesus, the apostles, and the New Testament prophets. Prophets today clarify and present the truth of Scripture in a powerful and culturally relevant manner. They call God's church to be all she is destined to become, even in the midst of a fallen world.

Evangelists

Alongside the laying of the foundation, the process also requires the role of *evangelist*. Evangelists are the people who have a supernatural ability to share their faith in such a way that, when people hear it, they come to Christ. They have a God-given ability to motivate people to respond to the gospel. We are all called to do the work of evangelism, but for many it doesn't come as a gift. Our best opportunities often occur as a result of exercising our gifts. For example, some of us practice evangelism by serving and then sharing our faith, while others reach out by hospitality that includes conversations about Christ. Evangelists gather raw recruits. The early church was birthed by the apostles, given teaching and direction by the prophets, and grew as the evangelists broadcast the Good News. Multiple conversions occurred as the church multiplied. Today, evangelists like Billy Graham and Luis Palau exemplify this ministry on a broad scale, while countless other lesser-known evangelists in each of our churches motivate the rest of the body. They lovingly and boldly proclaim the gospel everywhere they go.

Pastors and Teachers

The final people-gift mentioned by Paul joins two terms: *pastor* and *teacher*. *Pastor* literally means "shepherd," someone who gives oversight, someone who feeds, cares for, and gives direction. A teacher is someone who communicates the truth of God's Word in a systematic way. In order for spiritual health to remain and expand, both pastoring and shepherding must be present. Elders, pastors, teaching staff, and seminary professors now carry out this role in the body of Christ.

Apostles, prophets, evangelists, pastors and teachers—you may be wondering why we've taken time to look at each of their duties. These definitions are crucial because they spell out the role of leadership in the body of Christ. A failure to understand biblical leadership roles explains why so many Christians never experience holy transformation. If we misunderstand the divine roles given to leaders and the purposes behind them, we will not be able to access the grace they were intended to provide.

In the church today, cultural norms have so skewed the roles of leadership that the average Christian thinks that his responsibility extends little beyond coming to church and allowing the pastor or clergy to do what we would call "the work of the ministry." That may not seem like a big deal to you, but following that format will remove you from the very place where God's grace intersects with your heart. Follow along now as we look at the biblical role of leadership. Your willingness to accept and act on this truth from God's Word will determine whether or not you have positioned yourself to receive the grace God has intended for you.

Leadership

The role of leadership in the church has little to do with prestige or position. Leadership gifts have specific purposes. What's a leader's job? Leaders equip the saints (believers). Apostolic, prophetic, evangelistic, and pastor-teaching gifts exist to equip the saints.

Most of us have been brought up to think the pastor's job is to do the ministry. That thinking, in itself, hinders the church. In fact, 85 percent of all the churches in America have plateaued or are experiencing a decline in attendance, and by and large it's because they don't believe Ephesians 4 enough to actually practice it. The decline is not at all surprising given our understanding of who is supposed to do the ministry. An average pastor with reasonable amounts of energy can service the spiritual needs of between 75 and 100 people. If you are a high-energy pastor, you can directly relate to about 150 people before you have a nervous breakdown. If you are driven, obsessive-compulsive, and willing to work 90 hours a week, you can keep up with about 200 in your congregation. I know. I've been there, done that. Every time the phone rang I would jump here, jump there, jump everywhere. My unspoken, unexamined motto was: "I gotta be everything to everyone." I assumed it was my job to do the ministry. Little did I know I was killing myself and robbing God's people of the very opportunities He had designed to transform their lives.

I knew Ephesians 4, but I didn't practice it for the

first three or four years I was a pastor. I lived at a neurotic pace that nearly cost me my health. Now I know what I was actually doing—I was doing things that other people could do a lot better. As a result, I was acting as a grace barrier rather than a grace provider.

The leadership roles in the church focus on equipping the saints. The word *equip* in the original language means literally "to restore." It's a surgical term referring to the treatment of someone who has had a compound bone fracture. To equip means to put the bone back into alignment so that it can heal properly. The same word is used in the New Testament to describe the way fishermen mended their nets. They restored the string mesh for usefulness. William Barclay wrote of equipping, "The basic idea of the word is that of putting a thing into the condition in which it ought to be."[1] For a church to be healthy, for transformation to occur, we have to have an equipping mind-set.

But the wrong model is so deeply ingrained that people new to an equipping church often find themselves frustrated. At first, equipping seems to isolate the pastor, whom the old system assumed was accessible to anyone, at any time, for any reason. We regularly explain our church structure in the following way to those who question the pastor's absence in some functions: "It's not that we don't love you. It's that we love you so much we're not going to take ministry away from you. We love you so much that even though you think a pastor can do it better, we're going to let a layperson who is more gifted—who actually can do it in a better way—love you." Once the change is in place, people wonder what on earth they were thinking under the old church model.

Typical Roadblocks to the Equipping Model

As I was learning how to equip the saints instead of trying to do all the ministry myself, I had some predictable conversations. One day a member called. She was mad, in a sweet way. "I noticed that you didn't come to visit me in the hospital," she began. (I discovered later she had been in for minor outpatient surgery on a foot. Yes, I know there's only minor surgery when it's not your own, but on the relative scale of life-threatening procedures, hers was very minor surgery. I had not been notified about her date with the doctor.)

Before I could respond, she continued, "How come you didn't come?"

I said, "Well first, I didn't know about it." When I learned about the type of surgery I realized that was fortunate because I would have been tempted to say, "Frankly, sister, neither the procedure nor the time you were at the hospital warranted my being there." Remember, this conversation was taking place in the context of months spent casting the vision of equipping and training small group leaders with their responsibilities. We really wanted to help people understand that the pastor does not do all our spiritual stuff. The pastor equips us so that we get to do the life and the action. At this point in our church's history, we were just breaking through the old mind-set, but the message was still encountering occasional resistance. Enter this dear sister.

Since I realized that not knowing was probably not a good explanation in her eyes, I decided to turn this into a fact-finding mission. I began, "Let me ask you, are you in a small group?"

She said, "Oh, yes. They're wonderful!"

"Did anyone from your small group visit?" I asked.

"Every member of the small group visited me. I had visitors every day," she gushed. She had clearly made the "crisis" nature of her surgery known to her group and they had enthusiastically met her need. They had also felt it unnecessary to "call in the pastor."

I said, "Really?" hoping she would make a connection with the equipping plan.

She said, "Yeah—and they even provided food for five or six days for my whole family while it was hard for me to get around."

Inwardly, I was impressed and delighted. I made a note to encourage that small group leader. Then I said, "Ma'am, can I tell you something? The body of Christ just operated the way it's supposed to. Those who know you best responded in love and kindness to meet your need. That's exactly what we're trying to accomplish here at Country Bible Church."

She said, "Yes, but you didn't come." She wasn't going to give up the old idea easily.

I said, "My job is not to make sure that I pastor you. My job is to make sure that you get pastored well. You received more and better ministry than you could have ever received from me. Who knows you best? Me or the people in your small group?" Silence. She must have thought it was a rhetorical question.

I continued, "Did you have any deep conversations, and did they pray for you? Who knows more about your family's needs? Me or your small group?" More silence. "So, who do you think was really better equipped to minister to you? Me or your small group?" No comment.

Trying to lighten the mood, I asked, "And besides, who do you think cooks better? Me or your small group?"

She snickered, and I thought we'd turned the corner. Not so fast. Her long silence was punctuated by her closing comment, "But you still didn't come." Her exposure to the traditional but unbiblical model of the pastor doing all the ministry was so deeply ingrained that she still hadn't "gotten it."

It isn't easy to break old habits. We've been brought up in a world that believes somehow the pastor, the person who speaks, is supposed to accomplish everything else, too. The congregation to whom I preach knows me pretty well. My struggles illustrate my sermons. My gift mix is relational. If it were humanly possible, after a service, I'd sit down with every single person and have coffee. I would do the same with you after you end this book if I could. But if, through this book, God speaks to your life and you have a conversation with someone else, using your gifts in a way that helps them, then I will have succeeded in ways I may never know this side of eternity. A pastor's job is to equip regular people like you and regular people like me for the work of service. When we do that, holy transformation begins to really happen.

Equipping works. It can become the norm. I think of a recent new member in our church. He introduced me to his wife and family, and I noted that they were gradually becoming involved in the life of the church. His name was mentioned in ministry reports, and I knew he was discovering a place of service. Then I heard he had a bypass surgery while I was out of town. (Between you and me, bypasses don't sound like minor surgery.) So I wrote him a note, "Hey! I'm sorry I was out of town during the surgery. I hope you're doing well. Want you to know I've been praying for you."

I heard back from him sooner than I expected. These days, you get a bypass today; you run a marathon tomorrow. He was in church the following week and he buttonholed me after the service. He shook my hand and said, "Man, what are you doing?"

I said, "What do you mean, what am I doing?"

"Why are you spending your time writing notes to people like me? I know you love me. My small group was right there. My wife and kids are fine. You need to do what God's called you to do. You keep on equipping us. We're happy to care for one another."

He gets it. Now, do I still visit the hospital? Of course. But I do it on the basis of my relational network and I do it just like you do it. Friends and people I know. I have a spiritual responsibility for our elders and our staff. But God says when the leaders equip and the people understand the next point, transformation really begins to occur.

KEY 2
EVERY MEMBER IS A MINISTER

Verse 12 describes the reason leaders equip the saints. Members are trained. They know the Word. They develop and hone their life-skills. They discover and practice their spiritual gifts. They're restored in their personal lives so they can give to others. Why? For the work of service. The word *work* is translated in the New Testament as "ministry." It also gives us the word *deacon. Minister* shouldn't be a synonym for *pastor.* The ministers are we regular people. Pastors shouldn't have all the fun. The real action in the body of Christ is getting to see your gifts played out in teams of other believers and watching people's lives change.

I hope you are beginning to get the picture. Remember what Christ did when He defeated Satan? He "led captive a host of captives, and He gave gifts to men" (Ephesians 4:8 NASB). **Your spiritual gift is a reminder of your spiritual position in Christ.** God gives grace, not only through leaders but also through the actions of "regular" believers, using their spiritual gifts. Holy transformation, morphing, true life-change occurs in powerful, supernatural ways when believers know, understand, and actively use their spiritual gifts. That's why it's so important for leaders to equip God's people by instructing them about their gifts and providing them with help in finding places to practice those gifts. That's also why it is equally important for believers to actually be in on doing the work of the ministry so their spiritual grace-gifts are used. Let me give you a quick picture I think will pull all this together.

The best parallel I can give you is a football game. Now, I know I'm not actually a football player, but I've enjoyed a lot of sandlot football. You gather in the huddle and the player/coach/quarterback draws the next play in the dirt. "OK, Charlie, you go past the blue car, take a left at the bush and then go long. Pete, hook around the big pothole and stop. Joe, you block that big guy, 'cause he killed me last time." Naturally, like foolish young people, we played tackle football—no pads. My physique earned me a lot of time on the injured reserve list.

Have you ever analyzed the huddle? The huddle represents the gathering where you make plans, where you talk about strategy, where you get equipped and prepared for what you're going to do. A dynamic, effective worship service accomplishes the same purpose. It's a spiritual huddle. It isn't the action. Do you know where the action is? The action is where you work. The action is inside your home. **In fact, you are a minister!**

In our church we have a limited number of *pastors,* with very specific duties. But we have thousands of *ministers* at Santa Cruz Bible Church. I know one minister in our church who poses as an insurance agent. He's an undercover minister. He meets with leaders in the Silicon Valley, where he does Bible studies with people throughout the dot-coms. We have mothers posing as minivan bus drivers. They pile kids in for trips to soccer games, secretly praying for all the youngsters, putting tapes on in transit to place good stuff into their minds, and then sitting in the stands as equipped ministers, sharing their faith. We have members at HP, IBM, Plantronics, in cubicle after cubicle after cubicle. People think they just work there. They are actually ministers of the gospel. They carry on Bible studies in those places. And when they hear about a personal need or the breakup of a marriage or a child that has cancer, they move in and they represent Christ to those people.

Under God's plan for the church, every member is a minister. When you get involved in that ministering process, life gets downright exciting. You might say, "Hmm, I don't know how to do that. You're talking about these gifts. I don't know what mine are. In fact I've never been involved and I don't know if I'd ever be any good at helping someone else spiritually." Let me state this very plainly, every child of God has at least one spiritual gift. If you are a believer in Christ, the Spirit of God came into your life, if He didn't, you're not a believer. So if you have received Christ, the Spirit of God already lives in you. You were sealed with the Spirit, adopted into God's family, and forgiven of all your sins (see Ephesians 1:13–14). The Spirit of God dwells in you, manifesting the power and the presence of Christ. You have a spiritual gift.

Part of the adventure of the Christian life is *discovering and practicing* that spiritual gift. There are a number of tools available to help you recognize that gift. If you are unsure about how to discover your spiritual gift, ask your pastor for some direction. I encourage you to make it a point to be connected with the body Christ and discover your gift. Making yourself available to be used by God and allowing Him to develop and transform you into an effective minister —that's God's plan for you. As you learn to serve, care for, and love others by meeting their needs through your spiritual gifts, an amazing thing will begin to happen. The words of Jesus in Luke 6:38 will describe your experience, "Give, and it will be given to you. A good measure, pressed down, shaken together and running over, will be poured into your lap. For with the measure you use, it will be measured to you."

So, the question answered in this section is not whether you are a minister or not. It's just, Are you a good minister or a not-so-good one? An equipped one or a not-so-equipped one? One who is having a lot of impact or one who is having little impact? One who is passive or one who is giving out grace (and, as a result, receiving it as well)?

Key 3
Ministries Are Developed to Help Every Believer Live Every Day in Every Way Just as Jesus Would Live If He Were Living Out His Life in Their Body

Why? Why is it so important that leaders equip and everyone ministers? What's the goal? What's behind all this? Look at the principle listed above. Ephesians 4:13 tells us that, when people minister in the body of Christ, it's for these purposes. First, "until we all attain to the unity of the faith" (NASB). There's a sense in which you are connected to the body of Christ. Not just the faith, as in a common theology (ideas we share), but the faith as expressed by our unified walk with Christ together (the lives we lead).

The second purpose behind every member being a minister is the next line, "And of the knowledge of the Son of God" (NASB). The Greek word for "knowledge" here is significant. English is one of the few languages that can say, "I know you," and, "I know algebra," without distinguishing the kind of knowledge involved. The "knowledge" in Ephesians 4:13 is the word *ginōskō,* meaning "to know only by personal experience." Then, since the author wants to really let you know how powerful it is, he put a prefix to make it *epiginōskō,* meaning "a deep, personal, intimate knowing."

God's desire for every person in the body of Christ involves not only a unity of the faith when you come into the faith but also a genuine experiential knowledge of the Son of God that produces maturity. "To a mature man, a mature woman," writes Paul. This is the third purpose behind "every member a minister." The word for mature here is *teleios* from which we get *telescope.* The word refers to pattern or design. Used in this context, it means that you become all that you were designed to become—a new person in Christ.

The last phrase Paul uses points to the expanse or size of the pattern God is using: "To the measure of the stature which belongs to the fullness of Christ" (NASB). God's standard of maturity is Jesus Christ. The closer we come to being conformed to the image of Christ, the more our lives will be characterized by maturity.

In the next chapter we will look at a fourth key in God's game plan that focuses on results. We can actually know we are making progress in our spiritual journey as certain traits become more and more settled in our lives. We will do this by looking at how God measures spiritual maturity. He uses at least four specific criteria that indicate that holy transformation, the process of becoming more and more Christ-like, is actually occurring in your life and mine.

8
HOW TO KNOW IF
YOU'RE REALLY MORPHING

EPHESIANS 4:11–16

I had only been a Christian a few months. I honestly didn't know anything about the Christian life. A bricklayer in the community where I attended college took me under his wing. He began to meet with me weekly to teach me how to walk with Christ. He was low key, low pressure, and genuinely loving. I watched him interact with his wife and their four children, living out the beauty of their relationship in Christ as a couple and as a family. They weren't perfect and they didn't have it all together. But they were unforgettable models for me of holy transformation.

During the next eighteen to twenty-four months, Dave taught me how to read and study the Bible. He helped me begin to memorize two or three verses a week, setting the pace with his own personal reviews and continual Scripture memory work. He also introduced me to some of the classic books of the

Christian faith. Under his guidance, I began to learn how to verbalize my faith. We attended a Bible study with a group of men, where I watched my blue-collar mentor interact with other men across the social and educational spectrum, drawn together by their faith in Jesus Christ and their genuine care for one another.

I had never enjoyed church much, but I found myself eager to get up on Sunday mornings and attend worship on my own. Little by little, my outward activities were changing. People began telling me what a wonderful Christian I was because I was doing all the right activities. They certainly didn't know (nor was I eager to tell them) about all the struggles I was having inside my heart. No one saw the internal battle with lust that I was constantly losing in my mind. No one saw the skirmishes with envy, anger, and coveting that created daily defeats. Externally, I looked good, but over the next two years I fell into a spiritual trap that almost ruined my relationship with Christ.

It may sound strange, but what you don't know about morphing can really hurt you. Reading the Bible is crucial. Prayer is necessary. Participating in a Bible study is important. Church attendance also fits in the "high priority" category. "Cleaning up" some of those major external sins like profanity and angry outbursts has definite value, but they can easily lead others to conclude that parallel changes are also happening internally. Holy transformation is much more than eliminating old activities and taking up some new ones. In fact, if you are not careful, some of the means of holy transformation can become ends in themselves. The Bible calls that tendency legalism—settling for an appearance of righteousness when in fact our souls are a mass of sinful contradictions. Jesus' harshest words in all the New Testament were directed not to immoral sinners but to self-righteous religious people whose lives were filled with religious activity and external righteousness but whose hearts were far from God.

During the next two years I became immersed in Bible study, Scripture memory work, and various efforts to become the "ideal Christian." I received more and more praise from my college Christian group as I seemed, by external appearances, like an on-fire, high-impact, deeply spiritual young man living for Christ. But under the surface zeal of my life were hidden layer after layer of pretense, self-righteousness, and guilt. I remember feeling overwhelming guilt when I missed my quiet time. My prayers over time became little more than reciting lists of needs and requests—I couldn't go to bed until I made it all the way through my list. I couldn't bear to miss church, not because I wanted to be with God, but because I had a subtle need to be noticed there. In my mind I was judgmental of almost every Christian who I perceived was doing less, sharing his faith less, or not giving as much money as I was giving. Little by little I was transformed from my early joy and love for Christ into a self-righteous religious zealot.

I don't know if you can identify with this kind of Christian, but they are often acclaimed in our day as being very spiritual. These are the people who are more zealous than the rest of us and make sure that we know it. Their lives are filled with religious duties, but they experience very little delight in the Lord. They may complain of near-exhaustion as a result of their superhuman efforts in ministry, but when you get close to them you don't see much joy or sense much love. That's the kind of Christian I had become.

I'll never forget the day God began to reveal to me how far I was drifting from genuine transformation. I was walking across campus when I met a girl with whom I had become very good friends about three years earlier. She had watched the changes in my life from my earliest days as a Christian, and she could see the growing lack of genuine character qualities in me. I can still picture exactly where we had our "chance" meeting. We approached each other on the sidewalk between classes and stopped to talk. We had the open courtyard to ourselves for a few minutes as we stood in the bright autumn sun. After we exchanged pleasant greetings, she looked straight at me and caught me completely off-guard with her words.

"Chip," she began, "I remember when you were a really neat guy. When I first met you, you had a contagious joy, and you treated people like they really mattered. You were fun to be around. In fact, you were the first Christian I ever met who I wanted to be like!" Her phrases landed like a boxer's jabs to the chin of my empty spiritual life. Then she followed through with a knockout punch. "But that's not you anymore. No matter what people say, you always quote a Bible verse. There's an air about you that makes me feel guilty and bad—like I don't measure up—to you or to God. I don't know what happened to you, but I sure don't like it!" She didn't expect a response, and I had none to give. But she said one more thing before she turned away and left me standing in the sunlight alone: "If this is what it means to be a committed Christian, I don't know that I would ever want to be one."

I felt at that moment as if God had instructed that girl exactly how to verbally punch me to cause the maximum amount of damage to my bloated self-righteousness. That caring, non-Christian friend might as well have been an angel. She was a truthful mirror God put in front of me when I least expected it but desperately needed it. Unfortunately, as she walked away, I began to rationalize her words as the unfair and perhaps jealous expression of someone who wasn't even a believer. What right did she have to make statements about my spirituality? What did she know?

I wasn't about to surrender immediately to the truth, but I couldn't dismiss my friend's words. Her disappointment and honesty cut through my defenses. I had to admit she was right—my joy was gone. I wasn't a very loving person. Once the light of truth began to shine on my life, all I could see were huge mounds of guilt and my vain efforts to gain acceptance from God through my performance. I began to realize that I had made the approval of other Christians a cheap substitute for God's genuine love.

Though I hope I haven't been describing your story, experience tells me that many people reading these pages have lived or are living exactly the way I lived for those two years. You may well be someone like I was or know someone like I was who turned you off from New Testament Christianity because of the emptiness of his or her religious lifestyle. Whatever the case, it raises a fundamental question about holy transformation. **How do you know whether you are really spiritually morphing or simply going through religious motions?** In other words, how do we measure true spirituality? If we are being transformed into the likeness of Christ and God's Spirit is making us into a new person, how do we measure and verify that we're making progress? How can we be sure we're even on the right track?

What's great about Scripture is that God does not leave us in the dark on important matters like these. In fact, in our study of Ephesians 4:11–16, we learned that the first part of that passage provides God's structure for holy transformation—leaders equipping, members ministering, and all of us maturing into the likeness of Christ. Beginning at verse 14, we're told how we can actually measure our spiritual development. Notice how Paul states this:

> Then we will no longer be infants, tossed back and forth by the waves, and blown here and there by every wind of teaching and by the cunning and craftiness of men in their deceitful scheming. Instead, speaking the truth in love, we will in all things grow up into him who is the Head, that is, Christ. From him the whole body, joined and held together by every supporting ligament, grows and builds itself up in love, as each part does its work.
>
> EPHESIANS 4:14–16

In these three verses we can identify four distinctive signs that can be used to measure spiritual progress. Or to put it another way, in this passage God gives us the litmus test for true spirituality. To the degree that these four signs are occurring in your life and mine, we can know how spiritually mature we are actually becoming.

The startling characteristic about these signs is that they don't merely measure external activity. Let's not forget Jesus' own words in the Sermon on the Mount, declaring that our righteousness must surpass that of the scribes and the Pharisees (Matthew 5:20). In other words, it's not enough to be involved in church, to have a ministry, to know the Bible, and to clean up external areas of our lives. Religious, moral people may try hard to do these things, but they don't add up to holy transformation. **What we are talking about is a metamorphosis of the heart that grows out of a love relationship with Jesus and is empowered by grace and appropriated by faith.** So, let's look at these four signs and ask ourselves, "How are we really doing in this life transformation process?"

The First Evidence of Developing Spiritual Maturity: Doctrinal Stability

The first sign of developing spiritual maturity involves doctrinal stability. In other words, you have to have a settled knowledge of God's Word in order to grow. Growth can occur as God's Word forms the foundation of truth for your life. "As a result," Scripture says, "we are no longer to be children, tossed here and there by waves and carried about by every wind of doctrine, by the trickery of men, by craftiness in deceitful scheming" (Ephesians 4:14 NASB). The word *trickery* refers to skill in manipulating dice. Paul is talking about spiritual con men. When you become spiritually mature, you know the Bible— you know the basic teaching. When people knock on the door and want to give you literature and "new truth" about Christ, you can say with confidence, "That's not what God's Word teaches." Then you add, "Excuse me. What's your position on the deity of Christ? Where do you stand on the issue of the Trinity?" And when they say, "Well, I don't know. What do you think?" You pull out your Bible and say, "I know exactly what I think. Let me show you." In other words, frauds and counterfeit teaching don't suck you in.

That's the first sign of maturity—doctrinal stability. You see, it's not simply reading the Bible regularly so that you don't feel guilty or memorizing Bible facts that provides evidence of spiritual maturity. It's learning and understanding what God's Word says so that your faith is solid and strong, rooted in a clear understanding of your identity in Christ and His work on the cross for you.

Your personal devotion life is where you begin. You've got to read the Bible systematically and regularly, not as some dreaded duty to fulfill, but as a love letter to help you grasp and understand the wonder of your new relationship in Christ.

You can also think of it in much the same way you might approach a new, razor-sharp sword. The Bible describes itself in just such a way (Hebrews 4:12). It is as sharp as a well-honed sword. It has the supernatural ability to reveal the thoughts and intentions of your heart. The first time you pull a sword from the scabbard you are in greatest danger of cutting yourself. But leaving it safely sheathed (unopened) will leave you defenseless. Holy transformation demands that we get an accurate grasp of the Scriptures. And that takes time and discipline. There are no shortcuts. It means that you've got to make time to read it, think about it, apply it, and enjoy it. But remember: It's not an end in itself—it's a means of grace to cultivate your relationship with God. Expect to be awkward when you start. Practice will make you better. Find trusted teachers and books that can act as your instructors, but keep working and enjoying learning to handle your own sword.

THE SECOND EVIDENCE OF DEVELOPING SPIRITUAL MATURITY: AUTHENTIC RELATIONSHIPS

The second sign of developing spiritual maturity involves authentic relationships. Paul describes the content of authentic relationships. "Speaking the truth in love, we are to grow up in all aspects into Him who is the head, even Christ" (Ephesians 4:15 NASB). That's a commitment to both people and the truth, not just a commitment to people and the truth when it's convenient or when it works for you. In other words, you'll know you're genuinely maturing in Christ when you see a brother or sister in Christ who's moving in a direction that would be harmful to them or harmful for the body, and despite your fears you are committed to tell them the truth. You schedule a breakfast or a lunch or a coffee. You buy the refreshments and set the agenda. You prayerfully say:

- "I love you too much to simply stand by in silence when I see what's happening in your marriage."
- "I love you too much to not share with you what I see you're doing to one of your kids."

You practice your words, you pray, you get knots in your stomach, you don't sleep the night before, but you speak the truth in love. You're the kind of friend about whom they say, five years later, "If it wasn't for you, I would have shipwrecked my life." See? That's spiritual maturity. That's becoming like Jesus.

You also have people in your life who can speak the truth in love to you. After the encounter with my friend on the campus sidewalk, I remember going to my spiritual mentor and asking him if he saw any truth in those painful observations by my non-Christian friend. To my shame and initial pain, my mentor confirmed that pride, self-righteousness, and trying to please people were the most visible evidences of the true condition of my spiritual life. I was crushed! I couldn't believe that someone who was committed to helping me spiritually could say such hard and painful things to me. Later, I read Proverbs 27:5–6 and saw his honest words in a much different light. "An open rebuke is better than hidden love! Wounds from a friend are better than many kisses from an enemy" (NLT). My mentor had been waiting for a long time for just the right opportunity to tell me his painful comments. I look back now and realize that he loved me as few people have ever loved me in my life. He loved me enough to tell me what I really needed to hear, even if it meant putting our relationship at risk.

Let me ask you, how many people would call you that kind of friend? How many people depend on you to speak the truth to them in love? To what extent has that quality become part of your relationships? Do you have people in your life who have demonstrated their willingness to speak the truth in love to you? If not, make it a point to start looking. First, ask God to help you identify people in your life who may have been speaking the truth in love, but to whom you haven't been listening. Some of your relationships may get upgraded to being more loving than you thought! Carefully consider how you can apply Proverbs 27:5–6 more consistently with those closest to you.

Speaking the truth in love makes up the second litmus test of holy transformation in your life. It may actually be the most neglected sign of maturity in the body of Christ today. The absence of authentic, "truth-telling" relationships surely explains much of the appalling, widespread immaturity throughout the church in these times. We have Christians living with significant spiritual blind spots that are keeping them from knowing or reflecting the beauty of Christ in their lives and are also producing chaos and destruction in their relationships. And it's in large part because we are simply not willing to speak the truth in love. Spiritual metamorphosis of the supernatural variety always produces authentic relationships.

The Third Evidence of Developing Spiritual Maturity: Full Participation

The third sign of developing spiritual maturity involves full participation. Notice Ephesians 4:16a, "From whom the whole body being fitted and held together by what every joint supplies, according to the proper working of each individual part" (NASB). Three key words stand out for me: "whole," "every," and "each." You are one of the *each* individual parts, and your *every* relationship fits into the *whole* called the body of Christ. The phrase "fitted and held together" is a construction term describing how two boards can be hinged. It's the idea of a flexible attachment, exactly like the role of a ligament in your body. The body of Christ is a beautiful, complex, living organism, and you and I are pieces that need to fit together exactly where God wants us. The *whole* body can't be all it needs to be unless you're connected in that way. Full participation—you depend on the body and the body depends on you.

You see, spiritual maturity is impossible in isolation. No amount of Bible knowledge or devotional reading is a substitute for your finding your niche in a local body of believers. This is so important that Paul cites this kind of full participation as the third evidence of holy transformation. So let me ask you, are you connected in this manner in a local expression of Christ's body? Are you loving and being loved in a way that's "a good fit" with all concerned? If not, let me offer you some practical suggestions to help you. First, you have to get connected. Second, your gifts and talents need to be put into play in your local church. So, if you don't know your gifts, discovering them offers you an exciting adventure. In the meantime, service of almost any kind is a great place to begin. You can team up with other believers even before you know exactly what you have to offer.

What I often tell our church is, **"The most loved people around here are people who are involved in ministry."** Why? Because, when you minister to others, you get relationally connected and feel a part of what's going on. In the process of teaming up for ministry, you learn to pray and share honestly with one another, and you discover that others have the same struggles that you do. People who participate in the functioning of the body of Christ are demonstrating holy transformation. Their focus is not simply on their own needs but also on the needs of others. In fact, the very next phrase in our Scripture passage expands this thought by explaining why it's not enough to just be a participating member of a church, but that genuine participation leads to the highest and clearest evidence of spiritual transformation—love.

THE FOURTH EVIDENCE OF
DEVELOPING SPIRITUAL MATURITY:
A GROWING CAPACITY FOR LOVE

The fourth evidence of becoming spiritually mature is a growing capacity for love. Paul expressed this thought in his final phrase of verse 16, "causes the growth of the body for the building up of itself in love" (Ephesians 4:16b NASB).

But before you conjure up "ooey-gooey" emotional pictures of Christians sitting around campfires singing "Kumbaya," note that the term used for love here is *agape*—God's kind of love. Paul is not teaching that we know we're mature spiritually simply by our emotional responses or feelings toward others; instead, we know we are maturing spiritually when we evidence the same kind of supernatural love toward others that Jesus modeled for us.

I received a note from a friend not long after a sermon on Mark 4, which illustrates that the kind of love Paul teaches is a true indicator of our spiritual maturity.

Dear Chip,

Just wanted to say I got a lot out of your teaching concerning Mark chapter 4 and the application you made for the church. But I've made some personal applications on my own as I'm dealing with my cancer. Just as the disciples were in for an adventure as they were going over to the other side of the lake, likewise my cancer has become an adventure that the Lord is using for all sorts of good (Romans 8:28). I've had opportunities to **share my faith,** opportunities to **shepherd others,** opportunities for **teaching, witnessing,** growth in **relationships with my family** and those that I love, **depth in our growth group,** prayers abounding, **overflowing love,** as well as many other good and godly things. Meanwhile back home at the ranch, Vicki and I are doing fine. God is good all the time.

When you read that note, you may not think it is too profound, but I do. You see, my friend wrote me those thoughts when he was battling pancreatic cancer. He was literally within sight of death and had been told by the doctors he had no chance of living. I put in bold all the phrases in his note that show how his focus and concern was on others rather than himself. Here was a man experiencing spiritual metamorphosis with such intensity that in the midst of facing his own mortality he demonstrated a supernatural love by giving grace to his doctors, by sharing his faith with his nurses, and by bringing his family close to meet their needs. There was no inward focus or victim mentality. Instead, there was a supernatural, outward-directed, sacrificial attitude the Bible calls agape love—God's kind of love. Jesus taught and modeled for us that the greatest evidence of holy transformation is loving God and loving others.

At the end of the day, regardless of our spiritual background or practices, we can know how well we're doing in our journey with Christ by honestly answering a very clear two-part question: **Am I loving God**

more deeply as evidenced by my obedience (see John 14:21), and am I loving others more authentically? The degree to which we can answer that question in the affirmative is also the degree to which the Spirit of God is bringing about the miraculous work of holy transformation in our lives.

A TIME TO REFLECT

As we finish this chapter, I want to give you some time and some tools to reflect on what you have read. We've made some bold statements from Scripture about what it really means to be spiritually transformed. We've learned that morphing is not about church attendance, Bible reading, and external righteousness. We've learned that holy transformation will be evidenced by four clear signs whose development we can measure at any time in our lives. These signs were never meant to be a crushing weight over our heads to make us feel bad and guilty; nor were they given as a standard of comparison with other believers. Instead, they function as a light over our lives to help us follow the promptings of the Spirit of God as He works within us to make us into the people we long to become and that He designed us to be. In fact, we've learned from Ephesians 4:11–16 that God is committed to helping you and me become the persons He saved us to be, so much so that He's given gifted leaders clear instruction and supernatural power to help us reach spiritual maturity. God doesn't want people commenting some day on how religious we are or how impressed they are with our spiritual discipline. He longs for people to look at your life and mine and say,

- "He used to have a violent temper, but he's so kind now."

- "She used to be so vain and self-centered, but that's not the way she is anymore."

- "He used to be a loner and controlling and negative, but not anymore."

- "She used to be co-dependent and addicted to pleasing people, but all that has changed."

- "He was an alcoholic, and a drug addict, but now he's helping others escape the things that had a hold on his life."

- "She used to battle an eating disorder, but now it's not like that."

Can you hear them saying those things about you? "He's changed." "She's changed." Occasional slipping and imperfections, of course, will always characterize our lives, but we're different—really different—and we're different from the inside out.

Why? Because God longs to bring out the best in His children. And with that truth in view, let me ask you a very important question: **Are you positioning yourself in an environment where God can change you?** If you're not sure, I encourage you to carefully survey the diagnostic tool below. It will also help you develop a clear picture of your present stage of spiritual maturity. It will point out places where you are "out of position" when it comes to experiencing all that God wants to do in your life.

DIAGNOSTIC TOOL

Rank yourself (or better yet, ask a friend to help you rank yourself) on the scale from 10 percent to 100 percent in the following areas outlined in Ephesians 4:11–16.

1. I am currently involved in activities and training that are equipping me to do the work of the ministry.

Rarely	Sporadically	Consistently
10%	50%	100%

2. I am currently participating in intentional, meaningful, biblical worship on a regular basis.

Rarely	Sporadically	Consistently
10%	50%	100%

3. I am currently in an apprentice or mentoring relationship with an older believer that is stimulating my spiritual growth.

Rarely	Sporadically	Consistently
10%	50%	100%

4. I am currently ministering and building into the lives of others.

Rarely	Sporadically	Consistently
10%	50%	100%

5. I am becoming more like Christ in my everyday life, as evidenced by a desire to read God's Word, a disciplined study and understanding of God's Word, and an ability to see through false teaching.

Rarely	Sporadically	Consistently
10%	50%	100%

6. I am becoming more like Christ in my everyday life, as evidenced by enjoying one or more deep, authentic relationships in Christ.

None	1–2	3 or more
10%	50%	100%

7. I am currently in a small group where speaking the truth in love is common. I have three or four gut-level accountability relationships that are helping me through the most sensitive areas of my life.

Not currently	Hit and miss	Yes
10%	50%	100%

8. I am becoming more like Christ in my everyday life, as evidenced by a desire to become more deeply involved with God's people, to worship, to learn, to serve, and to meet the needs of others. I have a clear sense that I fit in the body of Christ. I am loved by others, and I find myself caring and helping them in increasing measure.

Rarely	Significantly	Yes
10%	50%	100%

Where are you in the transforming process? If you are a leader, are you equipping? If you are a member of the body of Christ, are you ministering? Are you growing in love? It's possible. God has made provision for it to happen to you and to me if we will place ourselves in the fertile soil of His grace. You can become the person you long to become. I invite you to use the prayer below as a starting point.

A PRAYER

Lord, thank You for the road map. I ask for the honesty to measure my spiritual maturity by Your criteria, not mine. I ask now for the courage and clarity to understand what the next step would look like. Please, give me the desire to put myself in a position where the Holy Spirit can equip me, where I can minister, and as I minister can begin to see Christ formed in others and in myself. I ask for Your help to make me doctrinally sound and relationally authentic. Help me fit in with Your plans for me in the body of Christ. I ask You, God, to do what only You can do. Make Your love grow inside me. I ask You to do this in my personal life and in the local body I attend, for Your glory. In Jesus' name, Amen.

9
WHY IS LIVING THIS NEW LIFE SO DIFFICULT?

EPHESIANS 4:17–24

There is one question I hear probably more than any other once I get beyond the casual introductions and really start to get to know people. It doesn't come immediately. We sit down, have a cup of coffee, and begin to share our mutual spiritual journeys. When it's their turn, they clear their throats, look around, and ask me the big question. I know it's coming. The specific words may vary from person to person, but almost invariably, when I am talking with someone in our culture who has been a Christian for a while, I hear the following introduction and question.

"OK. Look, Chip," they begin, "I've got it. I understand that I was a sinner, that I offended a holy God, and that Christ came and died for me and then He rose again from the dead. When He died on that cross He paid for my sin, OK?"

I suspect what's coming, so I just nod.

"And I know it's a gift—it's by grace we're saved through faith. And last month (or last year or three years ago or twenty-three years ago) I made a sincere decision. I heard the gospel and afterwards I put my trust in Christ and His work on the cross. I asked the Lord Jesus to come into my life. And I meant it. Afterward there was a sense of joy and peace. God began to move in my life, my desires began to change, and I really wanted to live for Christ. I started reading the Bible, and I learned that it is God's will for me to be pure and holy and become like Christ. I suddenly found this new conflict in my heart and in my life. I wanted to do what's right, but I kept doing stuff that was wrong. On my bad days I wondered, *Did I really mean that prayer? Does Christ really live in me?* And on my good days, when I was doing well and spiritually "on fire," I'd get to feeling a little smug and I wondered why other people didn't get with it . . ."

They sigh. I wait. Their big question will soon arrive.

When it comes, they ask the question as if they are heaving a huge millstone at me that they are afraid is going to fall back and crush them. "**How do I live a holy life?** I mean how do I actually live out this new relationship with God? I want to do what's right, and I've tasted God's presence in my life, but I feel like such a failure—with no end in sight."

I know their question. I also understand the underlying feelings of frustration and even guilt that motivates the question. My own spiritual experience shares similarities with theirs. I didn't grow up in the church, and I'd never read the Bible until I was eighteen. I began my Christian life with little more than my awareness of myself as a sinner and Christ as my Savior. I desperately struggled in the early months of my new relationship with Christ. I often felt so discouraged and guilty that I wanted to give up. Jesus had given me a new life, but I didn't know how to live it out. There were some caterpillar and cocoon habits of my old life that I needed to identify and leave behind as I lived my new life in Christ. But I didn't know how! At times, to be perfectly honest, I didn't want to know how! In order to live a holy life we need to recognize that we all bring the baggage of our old destructive lifestyles with us. And although the baggage and the struggles are normal, God has provided a way of deliverance.

How It Starts

The moment you pray to receive Christ you are declared righteous and placed in God's family forever. Then a process the Bible calls *sanctification* begins. That same grace that saved you starts to help you work out your faith in everyday ways. This sanctification process (or spiritual growth) progresses neither cleanly nor neatly. It's an uneven, messy process. Your loving Father begins to show you, in your everyday life, what it means to live in union with Christ. He is patient with you and me. He understands our ups and downs; our three steps forward, two steps back as we are gradually transformed into the likeness of Christ. Over time, your life changes degree by degree. God's Spirit begins to change your

thoughts, your actions, your speech, and your attitudes. The love of Christ moves you, and you become more and more holy and whole. I don't mean
holy like weird. I don't mean holy like you're going
to carry a really big black Bible, put a "Praise the
Lord!" bumper sticker on your car, and learn to be a
sort of judgmental, not-much-fun person to be
around. Though some people may think that's holy
living, that's not what the Bible teaches. Holy means
that you will become Christlike. You will be winsome and loving—transformed.

Too often, however, this process is oversimplified
(or worse) overspiritualized. I've read books and
heard speakers who make it all sound so easy and automatic. But the picture that the Bible gives of how to
become holy is a spiritual metamorphosis that is filled
with struggle. It's filled with tension. The same grace
that saved you through the gift of Christ on the cross
and His resurrection, is the same grace that empow-
ers you to say no to worldly passions and an ungodly
lifestyle. That grace teaches you progressively to say
yes to God and to live an upright, self-controlled, pure
life. Pure living in a sinful world is just plain hard, no
matter how you look at it. But such a life is possible.
And, better yet, we have all we need from God to live
that kind of life. If you are having a hard time grasp-
ing how this process of spiritual growth really works,
don't feel bad. It can be confusing. Sometimes a picture is worth a thousand words. Let me share the following parable, or picture, that has helped me to "get
my arms around" what living this new life looks like.

A PARABLE OF TWO BUTTERFLIES

Remember that picture in nature of a caterpillar, or worm, becoming a butterfly? Holy transformation works the same way. There is tension and struggle, but at the same time there's beauty and wonder. You and I have responsibilities in this journey toward holiness. Only God can change our lives, but we have a responsibility to team up with His grace in a way that brings about transformation. So how does it work?

I've developed a little illustration that I think will help you understand how to live a holy life for the right reason. I call it "The Tale of Two Butterflies."

This once-upon-a-time tale concerns two little butterflies, one named Barbara Butterfly and the other Barry Butterfly. Our heroes are sitting on a twig with their wings stretched out. The membranes are still a little wet, but a gentle breeze is drying their wings. They haven't taken off yet, but they're going to give flight a whirl in just a minute.

Barbara Butterfly says, "Oh, isn't it great? Do you feel the sunlight? Oh the joy! It's so good to be out of that cocoon. I can't wait to try this new adventure— and look down there. Flowers and trees, and I think we get to smell them and everything."

Barry turns to her and says, "Well, yeah, it is nice to be out of the cocoon, but you know, I knew what I was doing in the cocoon. I know it was dark and I know it was cold, but it also felt somehow secure. And by the way, I get dizzy when I look down. That's a pretty good drop to the flowers. How do you know these wings are really going to work?"

Barbara answers, "Watch!" She jumps off the leaf, and amazingly her wings respond as God created them. She does a few dips and rides a breeze here, checks out several flowers there, takes a climbing left turn, catches a gust of wind, whew! Right back, next to Barry. She breathlessly says, "Barry, it's beautiful! Everything. Better than I can say. In fact, Barry—the sunlight—it's coming through your wings. You're wonderful! You're beautiful. I wish you could see yourself. There's a whole world out there. **We've got a brand-new life!** We are not worms anymore. We're butterflies. We're new creatures. Oh, it's going to be so exciting!"

Barry shakes his head sadly and says, "You know, Barbara, I'm afraid of heights and I don't think I'd be a good flier. I mean, these wings kind of stick out and they're so obvious. What are all my worm buddies going to think if I actually start flying around? I'm not sure I'll have the same kind of relationships with them . . ."

Barbara nods, smiles, and says, "Well, Barry, after all, you are a butterfly. You're not a worm anymore."

Barry says, "Well, I know that's true, but let's just keep it between you and me." Then he folds his wings as much as he can, and he scooches to get as far back in the cocoon as he can. By now a few little maggots have taken up residence, so it's a little crowded.

Barbara tries one more time, "Barry, you weren't made to be in a cocoon. You were made to fly. Come on, let's go."

And Barry says, "Well, I know that and you know

that. I know this cocoon is dark and filled with worms, but at least it's home." He lies there, uncomfortable, half in, half out of his smelly, rotting cocoon.

So Barbara jumps off and takes flight to a brand-new way of life. Every time she uses her wings they get stronger and stronger. Her life's an adventure.

THE MORAL OF THE STORY

I know it's a silly little story, but it's a great picture of the struggle we all face after we've placed our faith in Christ. It also provides me with an opportunity to ask fellow believers an important question: **Which of those two butterflies most reflects your life?** Has your life since you trusted Christ been more like Barry's or Barbara's? Honestly, which of those two butterflies most reflects how you are living your life right now? Are you the kind of person who is really taking steps of faith? Are you the kind of person whose life is an adventure? Are you the kind of person who really knows what it means to live as a Christian? Or are you trying to figure out how you can be a Christian yet live as much in your old cocoon as possible? Here's the axiom of our parable: **A new life demands a new lifestyle.** That's the key to understanding growth and holiness. A new life demands a new lifestyle.

The Scriptures say in 2 Corinthians 5:17, "If anyone is in Christ, he [she] is a new creature [You're not a worm anymore. You're a butterfly.]; the old things passed away; behold, new things have come" (NASB). If you are a Christian and long to experience the beauty and power of your new life, then stay with me. If you honestly want to be more like Barbara Butterfly but know you're really living more like Barry, don't be discouraged. The following pages will help you not only grasp what you need to know but will provide practical instruction to help you become the person God created you to be. But before I explain God's plan to help you experience the new life you possess, I must warn you about two common spiritual pitfalls to avoid.

RECOGNIZING TWO SPIRITUAL PITFALLS

Christians through the centuries have struggled with two kinds of errors in this area of holy living. The journey to spiritual transformation travels on the road with a deadly pitfall on the right and a deadly pitfall on the left. If you get stuck in either of those pitfalls, you will not only fail to become holy—you'll never become whole. God's dream includes a "you" that reflects His character and also rejects that part of your old cocoon lifestyle that is spiritually destructive. How we treat people when our lives are dominated by sin is painful for them and hurtful to us. And we pass those lifestyle habits on to our kids. Some of us come to Christ with a history of relationship dysfunctions or shame-filled addictions. We can be brand-new believers in Christ but never sever those strings with the past that can bring death and destruction to ourselves and to others. Those strings will remain attached to our past until we recognize and deal with either of the two errors that have plagued believers over the centuries.

The First Pitfall: Moralism

As the church has tried to figure out what it looks like to be holy, the first repeated error has reduced the Christian life to what I call **moralism.** This practice often shows up within groups of well-meaning people in the church who really believe that holiness is important. They believe moral purity is a spiritual priority, and they are right—it is! But they look around the body of Christ and see a lot of people who claim to be Christians but whose lives don't match up. In their (often sincere) desire to get Christians to "live like Christians," they pervert what the Scriptures teach about grace. Concerned that people will abuse God's grace, they teach (explicitly or implicitly) that God only loves those who keep certain rules. And when people keep those certain rules, that means they're pure and holy. These moralizers set up a standard, a moral, or a new set of laws.

So you come into this new relationship with Christ and before long you hear, "OK, now that you're a Christian you need to do this, this, this, and that. And by the way, now that you're a Christian, you may not have known it, but don't do this, don't do that, and for goodness' sake stay away from that other thing." The rules vary from group to group. They nearly always focus on external areas that are easy to measure and keep track of, such as how someone dresses or how often someone reads the Bible, goes to church, or prays. They even focus on what you can eat or drink, or what you must not eat or drink.

The results are disastrous. Those of us who come to Christ and begin to experience the wonder of His grace are met by a whole new world we didn't know existed. Before long, weight after weight is placed on our shoulders about what we ought to do, when we ought to do it, and how we must do it. People who are presented to us as spiritual leaders define for us what the standards of the Christian life are to be for everyone and in various ways enforce those standards on the group. Well-meaning and naive new Christians try very hard to keep all the new rules, thinking it's their expression of their love for God. But it doesn't take long for them to get frustrated, feel guilty, and realize that they can never measure up. I know. I've been there. After a while, many people in these kinds of groups either leave the Christian faith in quiet despair or simply begin to fake that they are keeping the rules. Both solutions are spiritually destructive. Both are symptoms of the first pitfall.

There are a few strong-willed people in these groups who eventually become like the Pharisees of Jesus' day. They keep the rules better than other people, and they walk around in a fog of self-righteousness. They become the kind of people we hate to be around. Their noses are slightly tilted in the air. They read the Bible rigorously and frequently remind us that they are faithful. They pray long prayers and leave us with the impression that they never have a bad thought. They have never watched an R-rated movie, have never uttered a cuss word, and certainly have never dealt with lust or coveting. Or so they would have us believe.

Here's the real situation. The internal lives of these people often reveal greater and deeper spiritual struggles than we could imagine. Though they appear as pure as the wind-driven snow, their purity has no depth. In fact, the moralistic pitfall that they teach and which swallows so many others eventually swallows them, too.

My heart breaks when I watch old and new Christians attempt to live a holy life through this perversion of Scripture. They start with a new life in Christ and understanding that it is all by grace through faith, but it rapidly degenerates into a joyless, humorless life of hard work and tiptoeing along the straight and narrow. There's no room for error. There's no room for adventure. Somewhere along the way, things get so narrow and defined that there's no more room for Christ. The beauty and delight of their new sonship in Christ is eventually traded in for the dry and mechanical duties of a slave. The Christian life shifts from a grace-filled relationship with Christ to the drudgery of a never-ending effort to keep the rules.

So, how about you? Do you feel more like a son or daughter who is deeply loved by God, or like a slave sentenced to a stern set of rules, regulations, and restrictions?

The Second Pitfall: Antinomianism

There is yet another group that starts with the observations we've just made, but arrives at an equally wrong conclusion. They see all these rules and say, "That's not what the Christian life's about! It's about relationship, not regulations. It's about grace; it's about God; it's about freedom." These people are called **antinomians.** That's a long word, but not that complicated. *Anti* means "against." *Nomos* is the Greek word for law. These are people who are against laws.

Even in the early church there was a group that started out right, then detoured into this ditch of antinomianism. They affirmed, "We are saved by grace, through faith." In that, they were correct. They continued, "Therefore, we're out from under the law. There's no standard, and there are no restrictions. It's great." They even quoted the apostle Paul: "Where sin abounds grace super-abounds" (paraphrase; see Romans 5:20). "So we have a great application," they proclaimed. "The more we sin, the more grace God pours out."

This pitfall was yet another perversion of God's grace, but this time in the opposite direction. The antinomians reasoned, "We know we're going to heaven because it's a gift from God, not of works." They went on to conclude, "We know God loves us totally apart from our performance. So we're going to give license to our lustful passions and let His grace really shine!" They not only sinned but openly flaunted their sinful behavior. Their logic was simple: "There are no moral standards. After all, we're free!" Unfortunately, their brand of freedom simply meant a detour back into bondage to old desires and wrongdoing.

The apostle Paul wrote to the antinomians in Galatia. He told them, "For you were called to freedom, brethren; only do not turn your freedom into an opportunity for the flesh, but through love serve one another" (Galatians 5:13 NASB). Yes, we're free from the law but bound to a higher law, the law of love. So, how does this affect you? Have you, in the name of "freedom in Christ" and "grace," gone back to your former desires and behaviors that were yours prior to coming to Christ? To what degree have you rationalized away any standards concerning what happens with your mind and your body?

THE QUESTION THAT REMAINS

These two errors raise a crucial question. If one pitfall in the world is trying to keep all the rules (and if you keep them you become self-righteous and if you don't you feel guilty and condemned) and the other pitfall is to blow them all off (and the results don't reflect the character of God or the Scriptures), how then do you become holy? What's God's way to holy transformation? How does it work?

THE ANSWER TO THE
PITFALLS AND THE QUESTION

A believer whose life does not change is an oxymoron. To be a believer is to have your life changed. If your life is not changing at all, you had better go back and find out whether you're really a believer. Genuine believers experience life-change. To become a butterfly there's got to be some change. You are not a worm anymore. You've left the cocoon behind.

God doesn't call you and me to try harder. God calls us to a new life with a new lifestyle. He desires for us to live consistent with who we are in Christ. We're not trying hard to earn God's favor (moralism). Nor are we practicing some vague, mental spiritual gymnastics where we say, "Well, I prayed some prayer after someone talked to me about grace. I did what I was told to do. I'm not actually living any differently but you know, the good news is that guy told me I'm going to heaven 'cause I prayed the prayer." If that is the sum of our faith, we've probably missed something along the way.

Let's look together at Ephesians 4:17–24, the next passage in our study of the fourth chapter of Paul's letter. That's where we'll learn how to live a holy life. These verses will guide us to the right way between the pitfalls and into a life of holy transformation.

> So I tell you this, and insist on it in the Lord, that you must no longer live as the Gentiles do, in the futility of their thinking. They are darkened in their understanding and separated from the life of God because of the ignorance that is in them due to the hardening of their hearts. Having lost all sensitivity, they have given themselves over to sensuality so as to indulge in every kind of impurity, with a continual lust for more.
>
> You, however, did not come to know Christ that way. Surely you heard of him and were taught in him in accordance with the truth that is in Jesus. You were taught, with regard to your former way of life, to put off your old self, which is being corrupted

> by its deceitful desires; to be made new in the
> attitude of your minds; and to put on the new self,
> created to be like God in true righteousness and
> holiness.
>
> EPHESIANS 4:17–24

The apostle Paul begins with another challenge: "So I tell you this, and insist on it in the Lord (very strong language—here's the command), that you must no longer live as the Gentiles do (Gentiles stands for pagans, the unbelieving world. Well, how do they live?), in the futility of their thinking (or in the futility of their mind) (4:17). The word "futility" here means "vain, aimless, purposeless, totally unrelated to God."

Next he's going to describe what the futility of an unbelieving mind looks like. "They are darkened in their understanding and separated (or alienated) from the life of God" (4:18a). Why? "Because of the ignorance that is in them due to the hardening of their hearts" (4:18b). Paul insists that it doesn't make sense for those who know Christ to live as if they did not know Christ. Then he fills in the picture of what it means to live with a darkened heart. "Having lost all sensitivity, they have given themselves over to sensuality so as to indulge in every kind of impurity, with a continual lust for more" (4:19). He is saying, in effect, "Believer, that old life I just described of people who have stiff-armed God, who have turned away from God, who are headlong into sensuality at all different levels—don't live the way you used to live!"

Now notice the positive contrast. "You, however, did not come to know Christ that way" (4:20). In other words, "When you metamorphosized, when you were born a second time, when you were born spiritually, you were told from the start that a radical life-change would be part of the process. Remember? You were told to count the cost." He continues, "Surely you heard of him (the preaching of the person of Christ) and were taught in him (you learned about how to grow and who He is) in accordance with the truth that is in Jesus" (4:21). This is a rare verse. It mentions Christ and Jesus in the same sentence, separately. Paul's intention seems to be to highlight the role and title (Christ/savior) as a way of reminding the Ephesians that meeting Jesus isn't like meeting anyone else. The results are life-transforming.

Paul goes on to review the content of what they were taught regarding the ways in which their new life in Christ would be different from their old lives. He's reminding them because some people in the Ephesian church who had apparently genuinely come to know Christ were now falling back into their old immoral lifestyles. "You were taught, with regard to your former way of life," (point number one) "to put off your old self, which is being corrupted by its deceitful desires;" (point number two) "to be made new in the attitude of your minds; and" (point number three) "to put on the new self, created to be like God in true righteousness and holiness" (4:22–24). The caterpillar in the cocoon is shedding the old form and putting on the new one. As Barry Butterfly illustrated earlier, the change has occurred even if the one changed doesn't recognize it yet. Paul points out that God-likeness (holy transformation) will look like righteousness and holiness in our lifestyles.

REVIEWING PAUL'S ANSWER

Three major points emerge from the passage we just surveyed. The first two instruct us as to why we must live a holy life. The third (which we will cover at length in the next chapter) lays out the details of how we can live a holy life. The principles Paul gave the Ephesians still function today. God has never stopped morphing people into His likeness.

Point #1: As Believers We Must Lead Lives That Are Progressively Characterized by Moral Purity.

Paul raises a challenging standard. As believers, we must lead lives that are progressively characterized by moral purity. This direction in a Christian's life is not an option or a maybe. As a believer, your new life in Christ demands that you live a different way. This change doesn't happen *in order* to earn God's favor (moralism), but *because* of who and whose you are. You have been changed (*who*) and you no longer belong to the world but to Christ (*whose*). Let's take a closer look at verses 17–19. This is one passage you should mark in your Bible.

> So I tell you this, and insist on it in the Lord, <u>that you must no longer live as the Gentiles do</u>, (in the futility of their thinking). They are (darkened in their understanding) and (separated from the life of God)[because of the ignorance that is in them] [due to the hardening of their hearts]. Having **lost all sensitivity,** they have given themselves over to **sensuality** so as to indulge in **every kind of impurity,** with a continual **lust for more.**
>
> EPHESIANS 4:17–19, notations added

I've made some notations in the text above that might help you develop a way of seeing the details in the Bible text. Note the underlined phrase "that you must no longer live as the Gentiles do." You might want to write the word *command* in the margin of your Bible next to that phrase. I've placed a parenthesis around each of the phrases that describe how the Gentiles live, "in the futility of their thinking," "darkened in their understanding," and "separated from the life of God." Write *state* in the margin, indicating the situation or position of those who have not responded to the gospel. These phrases outline a condition more like a dead-end than a passing phase. These people will not be able to think their way out of it nor intuitively figure out their predicament because they have become separated, excluded, or estranged from intimacy with God. They are mentally and spiritually blind.

This kind of harsh description naturally provokes the question "Why?" Paul has an answer. He begins his next statement with "because." I've used square brackets around the two phrases "because of the ignorance that is in them" and "due to the hardening of their hearts." Jot down the word *reasons* in the margin. The cause isn't intellectual ignorance in them. This is moral ignorance that characterizes a hardened heart. It's a picture of people who have become as hard as petrified wood toward God. Asking them to even think about God is like asking a rock to feel.

Children naturally exemplify softness of heart. They are open, inquisitive, and eager. They don't have a hard time seeing that God's creation gives testimony of the reality, the beauty, and the love of God (see Romans 1:18–20). They see a sunset and ask a delightfully honest question, "I wonder who made that?" When they see a little kitty born, they notice the wonder and the beauty of life. When they see people love one another, they grasp that that's what life is really all about. They readily receive these little messages about God and about Christ and about love and about reality.

But inside each one of us, even as children, is also a fallen state—the part that wants me, my, and mine. That part of us wants to see ourselves rather than anyone else at the center of the universe. It struggles against the obvious clues of God's presence. We hear God's voice and we stiff-arm Him. What a sense of power! We don't have to recognize God. Somewhere deep inside we begin to develop a resistance to God's voice and a blindness to God's presence. Our minds get darkened—meaning we can no longer hear God's voice or sense clues about His presence. We're alienated from Him because of our moral ignorance and the result is we don't know right from wrong anymore. We resisted what we earlier knew to be true. That's the reason the Scripture can state the indictment against every one of us, "For all have sinned and fall short of the glory of God" (Romans 3:23).

Paul includes one more category in his description of the human predicament. I used bold for the phrases "lost all sensitivity," "sensuality," "every kind of impurity," and "lust for more." In the margin write the words *applied results*. These phrases describe the lifestyle of those who are stranded in darkness apart from God. Paul went through all this to underscore his command to believers: "Don't live this way!"

The idea behind "lost all sensitivity" has to do with becoming callous. It's a picture of someone who does hard manual labor and develops calluses on his hands. You can stick a pin right into his finger, but the calluses are so thick he doesn't feel it. In a spiritual sense this describes someone who ceases to feel any pain or any great grief when he sins against God or others. He moves toward total moral abandonment. "Sensuality," "impurity," and "lust" indicate the natural progression that occurs when someone becomes callous to God's voice. These words form a composite picture of someone who's under the complete control of sensual, passionate lusts that are themselves out of control.

The world Paul described two thousand years ago is the world we live in today. Those who use the Internet know they don't have to look for pornography; it comes looking for them. Like all temptations, pornography boils down to a continual "lust for more," as the apostle so aptly put it. It's the surrendering of ourselves with all our passions, with gusto, with no regard for whom it may injure or hurt. There is no longer shame and there is no remorse. Now that's a pretty ugly picture of what happens to people who reject God.

It is important to remember, however, that this process is subtle. It involves a gradual rejection of the truth and what we know to be right. When a person first sins, there may be a short-lived thrill, but there also enters into the heart remorse and regret. But if the person continues in sin, there comes a time when he loses all sensation and can do the most shameful things without any feeling at all. His conscience has become petrified.

Sin is really just a broad picture of what happens to people who abuse drugs and alcohol or become entangled in sexual addictions. The second "hit" is never as good as the first, and it takes more to reach the same buzz. Soon it takes more and more just to keep the pain and intense desire at bay.

The progression and pattern is one that we've all wrestled with to a certain degree. In this text, the apostle describes in graphic detail how our rejection of God and our indulgence in sin eventually swallows and consumes us. Unfortunately, sin's power is so deceitful and subtle that we are gradually swept into the middle of its torrential flood and in danger of going over the waterfall of destruction before we recognize the danger we're in. No one ever woke up one day and said, "You know, I'd like to become a sex addict today. I'd like my mind to be dominated every moment with sexual images and thoughts. I'm going to arrange my life, my finances, everything, around finding a computer or an adult bookstore somewhere so I can somehow keep from thinking about my shattered life." No, it's a slow, deceptive process.

That same slow, deceptive process happens with material things. We neglect our spouse and kids because down deep we've concluded that some possession, position, or achievement will make us a "someone." We say, "When I get that car, honey, everything will be great. Yeah, we'll have time for the kids later; we'll buy a new home, take great vacations, etc." Or, "Boy, this big deal's got to come through. When that happens, then we're going to expand, and afterwards we'll work on our marriage and go back to church." I can't tell you the number of men that I know who have everything in life except what really matters.

Just recently a very successful businessman confided to me, "Chip, I did the whole nine yards. I had the house in Vail. I had the condo on the beach. I had the great house here. I drove nice cars, parked in the president of the company's space. We went public, and I had it all. I was a believer, but I lied to myself about what I was doing, why I was doing it, and what it was really costing me. Now I've lost everything, including my wife and my kids and most of my friends." I can see the apostle Paul shaking his head and saying sadly, "Live like the world, brother, and suffer the world's consequences." But it doesn't have to be that way. In fact, Paul is saying to believers then and now that a new life demands a new lifestyle.

Point #2: An Immoral Lifestyle Is Inconceivable for Us as Believers.

Holiness is about God making you whole. He wants to save you out of a destructive pattern that not only breaks His heart and embarrasses His family when butterflies live like worms, but will also destroy you. This is a loving God. His call to holiness isn't about random rules. God's commands say, "Let me protect you from yourself."

Unless we decisively choose to turn from sin and obey God's call to holy living, we will always err to the side of wrong. We will find ourselves all too easily rationalizing and compromising. Can you imagine what it would sound like if we put into words what our behavior so often reflects? "Well, Lord, why is it such a problem to have just a little immorality?" Or "Father, how about coveting in moderation? What about reasonable dishonesty?" We laugh when we read such ridiculous statements in print, but I have certainly lived periods of my life where a little immorality, some reasonable dishonesty, and mild coveting were the norm rather than the exception for me. So why is it so preposterous to seek to negotiate with God when it comes to spiritual purity? He answers those very questions and attitudes in verses 20 and 21. "You, however, did not come to know Christ that way. Surely you heard of him and were taught

in him in accordance with the truth that is in Jesus"
(Ephesians 4:20–21).

God's Word states categorically that an immoral
lifestyle is inconceivable for us as believers for two
reasons. First, because immoral living by a believer
contradicts who we are. We aren't what we used to
be. We're new creatures. Butterflies can't crawl like
worms! Butterflies have to fly.

Second, immoral living by a believer is inconceivable because it **contradicts who Christ is.** Notice again what the verse says, "You, however, did not
come to know [or learn] Christ that way" (4:20a).
The tense of the verb indicates a specific point in
time when you met Christ personally. He continues,
"Surely you heard of him [Remember the preaching?
Remember when you heard about him? Remember
when your heart was strangely warmed? Remember
that night or that day when you prayed to receive
Christ and it was so real?] and were taught in him"
(4:21a). You knew who He was. You know about
heaven. You've been told about the life. You know
about empowering by the Holy Spirit, you know
how it works. You know about His power. "In accordance with the truth that is in Jesus" (4:21b)
underscores Paul's point. That little phrase "in Jesus"
is very rare in the New Testament. It's a reference to
the historical Jesus. He's recollecting, "You've heard,
and you've been taught of who Jesus really is—the
life He lived. You were not attracted to some evil person; you were attracted to someone who lived a perfect
life. You were attracted to someone whose teaching
brought you life and peace. He taught about loving

people and about being salt and light." So Paul says to them and to us, "It's inconceivable to live an immoral life and claim to be a faithful follower of Jesus."

Let's summarize. First, your motivation for holy transformation is not brownie points with God. You are loved right now as much as you could ever be loved. It's eternal, infinite, and totally unrelated to your performance. If you have trusted Christ, you have been saved and cleansed and forgiven by the grace of God. This is your motivation: A good moral life is simply the natural by-product and reflection of a genuine, loving relationship with God. He unconditionally loves you, then manifests His character to others through you. This results in tremendous peace and joy within you, as well as harmony and intimacy in your relationships with others. God allows you to taste a little bit of heaven on this earth. It's consistent with who you are now, since you're a new creature. And it's consistent with who Christ is.

Do you get it? As long as the motivation is "God loves me when I'm good and He's down on me when I'm bad," you will forever be doing continual penance and living a very unproductive life. You will be spending most of your time either feeling very guilty or self-righteous. And guess what you will have missed along the way. **The relationship!** You will have missed God. You'll miss out on the wonder, beauty, and joy of Jesus in you, the hope of glory!

Now that we have recognized the reality and danger of continuing in our old, destructive lifestyle, let's turn in the next chapter to God's guidelines for breaking out of such a predicament. Hang on! Help is on the way.

10

THE PROCESS OF MORPHING: HOW TO BREAK OUT OF A DESTRUCTIVE LIFESTYLE

EPHESIANS 4:17–24

F rankly, I hope your frustration level has elevated a little. If you are typical, I can almost hear you saying, "OK, OK, Chip. I'm getting it. Or at least I think I'm getting it—but how? You know . . . how? How does holy transformation happen? How does this play out in my life and in my relationships? What do I need to know, or do, or understand to break out of those destructive behaviors of my past and experience God's power and presence on a daily basis? **How do I win the battle when . . .**

- it's late, and I'm tempted to go online where I don't belong?

- the book that I'm reading right now is so steamy that I put a different cover on it?

- I find myself lusting for the person in the cubicle next to mine at the office?

- I struggle with the secret desires I have?

- I get up and the first thing I do is grab my palm pilot to look at the stock market and check how we're doing—because I'm so driven by stuff?

- my mouth and my temper "spew out" sarcasm and destructive comments to those around me?

- my marriage and family are in ruins, and I don't even know where to begin to rebuild my life?

If these statements echo some of your thoughts and struggles, the apostle Paul has good news for you. Holy transformation is not just a nice idea or a lofty goal. It is God's answer to deeply flawed people in desperate situations. Spiritual metamorphosis is the solution even when we think there's no hope and nowhere to turn. God has actually given clear instructions about how we can experience His miraculous work in us.

THREE PRINCIPLES OF HOLY TRANSFORMATION

We achieve personal purity by following God's threefold principles of transformation. These are given to us in Ephesians 4:22–24: "You were taught, with regard to your former way of life, **to put off** your old self, which is being corrupted by its deceitful desires; **to be made new** in the attitude of your minds; and **to put on** the new self, created to be like God in true righteousness and holiness." The first principle deals with the past, the second with the present, and the third with the future. Empowered by the grace of God, all three combine to produce holy transformation.

First Principle: Put Off the Old

Paul begins his review by dealing with the past: "You were taught, with regard to your former way of life, to put off your old self, which is being corrupted by its deceitful desires" (4:22). The apostle is using a metaphor. He's literally saying, "Take off the ragged and shabby clothes of your old life. Quit wearing that old cocoon like a coat—take it off and cast it aside." The tense of the verb is decisive; it's a point in time. It's not that you gradually ease into holiness. Transformation doesn't work that way. You know it and I know it. He's saying there's a line to be crossed, a decision to make: I'm a new creature in Christ—I leave the cocoon life behind me. I decide at a point in time to put off the old. I don't go to those websites anymore. I don't read those books any more. I no longer hang out with those people that keep me doing things that I know are wrong. I don't visit the bars. I don't set out to pick up women or men. I don't do what I used to do. I clearly see my old life, and I turn away from it. That's the first step into holiness—**an intentional decision to leave your old life behind you.**

A lot of Barry Butterflys in America call themselves believers. I've been a Barry, so I know the life. Many of the Barrys come to church on Saturday night or Sunday morning, but they hit the bars on Friday. They feel a little bad about their hypocrisy, tell God they're sorry, but then unconsciously or consciously plan their week around their next visit to happy hour on Friday night. We call that life a vicious, self-destructive cycle for a reason—it eats you up inside.

I know. The first two years I was a Christian, I straddled the fence trying to live a double life. My experience and observations tell me that the most miserable people on the planet are people who are genuine believers who continue to live in known sin. Do you know why? When you live that way, you're in no-man's land. Your life is a "catch-22." As a believer, the Spirit of God now lives within you and you can no longer enjoy sin. The Spirit bears witness with your spirit that what you are doing is wrong. Sin's pleasure is overshadowed by a guilty conscience. This is what I discovered. As an unbeliever, sin was fun. After trusting in Christ, every time I sinned I grieved the Holy Spirit and experienced guilt and shame. Sin ceased to be fun. Sin lost its payoff, even though my desire to sin continued. Unfortunately, because I was continuing to live in known sin, I could not enjoy sweet fellowship with God. My prayers seemed pointless and ineffective. The effects of God's Word were dulled in my life. I lived a fake and superficial life when I was with other believers.

When we live a double life—on the fence—we are the most miserable of all people. Life does become a vicious cycle. Even as you read these words you may be painfully and intimately aware of what I'm describing. In fact, you may be living on the fence right now. You may know what it's like to feel overwhelming guilt, yet return to sin again and again until you feel desperately trapped. Believe me, God loves you too much to leave you there. Know for certain that the consequences of those sins will continue to multiply and bring pain and destruction to you and others. This may be the most important section of this book that you will read. Right now, the Spirit of God is saying to you, "Put your old life behind you! Make a willful decision right now that you will take off your 'old clothes,' put the old cocoon-life behind you, and from this moment move ahead in your relationship with Christ."

What do you need to put off? What are the old clothes of your old life? Is it materialism? Is it a "me-first" mind-set? Is it stuff that you watch or the movies you attend? Are you putting things in your mind on a regular basis that keep drawing you back to the lusts of the world? Most of you reading these words know what these things are—but if you don't, are you willing to let God point them out to you? Would you be willing to bow your head right now, ask the Holy Spirit to search your heart, and then sit quietly while He does that? Are you willing to ask God to bring you completely out of denial and allow you to see yourself and your motives for what they are? He wants to heal, forgive, and help you take off the old in order to put on the new.

Second Principle: Be Renewed in Mind

Paul next says you need to "be made new in the attitude of your minds" (4:23). Notice the present tense of the verb, which actually means "be continually renewed." I'm not highly technical, but I'm learning how to do some amazing stuff with my new computer. I share that because computers provide a vivid picture of how our minds are renewed in holy transformation.

Think of yourself as a computer for a moment. Here's what you have to do in order to put off the old. You've got to look at your previous life, place it all in one file, then click delete. Then, check your programs and you will discover that you have to get a new piece of spiritual software installed called Holiness/Walking With Christ. You've got to load it up on the computer of your mind. How do you do that? It means you've got to input the Scriptures by reading them. You've got to input positive relationships by being around believers. You've got to input honesty by getting involved in a small group where real accountability can take place. You've got to input network connections by hanging around with people who are winsome, holy, godly, and authentic. The Scriptures are clear—you're going to end up a lot like those with whom you hang out. Does that mean you forsake your old friends? No. It means you meet them on neutral turf or on your turf, not on their turf anymore. And in those areas that you are tempted, you don't go there anymore. Might you lose a friend or two? You might. But you might lose yourself if you don't. You've got to get your mind and heart reprogrammed.

Computers have default settings—their standard operating functions. You want your life default setting to be holy transformation. Your outlook continually returns to its basic settings. You say, "Since my new life is about Christ, I'm going to talk with God on a regular basis. I'm going to arrange and prioritize my life around becoming more like Jesus. I'm going to practice purity. I'm going to program my mind with stuff that takes me in the direction of integrity and love. I'm going to spend time with people going in the same direction I want to travel." Whatever the immediate activity you're involved in, you expect to have the background program of holy transformation always up and running. You will find your whole life orientation becoming more and more directed by the Holy Spirit so that, in a very personal way, what Paul told the Colossian Christians, "And whatever you do or say, let it be as a representative of the Lord Jesus, all the while giving thanks through him to God the Father" (Colossians 3:17 NLT), will be your heart's desire.

Basic Bible study and discipleship training is about reprogramming your thought processes. The way of holiness isn't crowded, but you will discover you're not alone. A few great spiritual traveling companions can make all the difference. Every command Paul gives in these verses is in the second-person plural. It's not you doing it alone with God. It's us walking on this journey of transformation together. There is great teaching available on all the aspects of the Christian life: how to study the Bible, how to pray, how to enjoy spiritual fellowship, how to share your faith. You and I don't have to re-invent the wheel when it comes to walking the road of winsome purity and joy. Others have been along here before and have left plenty of help for us.

Third Principle: Put On the New Self

The next step then is to "put on the new self," or put on the new clothes. It's a willful decision to make your focus, your goal, and your future all directed toward becoming a man or a woman of God. "Putting on the new self," means living with a new orientation that makes your relationship with Christ the central aspect of all that you are and all that you do. Christ will be reflected in how you do your job, how you handle marriage or live out your singleness, and how you parent your children. In fact, how you live, what you think, and what you feel will all be informed by your new relationship with Jesus.

Perhaps a snapshot from my own life would be helpful here. I made some drastic decisions shortly after becoming a Christian to make a break with my old life and "put on" the new life. Looking back, the changes don't seem all that major, but at the time they were the biggest steps of my life. They got me off the fence. They forced me to plant both feet in the land of personal purity and integrity. Holy transformation doesn't creep in—it begins with sudden decisions and often in crises.

One of the early crises in my life had to do with relationships. Coming to Christ in the midst of the early seventies' sexual revolution involved some immediate difficulties. At the college I attended, the girls outnumbered the guys by four to one. The temptations seemed overwhelming. In honest moments, I realized my mind was dominated by lust. My relationships with the opposite sex were anything but healthy. After living "on the fence" for two years and experiencing the internal trauma of guilt and failure, I made a drastic decision to treat the opposite sex in a way that would honor God.

I made some very practical decisions that not only made a break with the past but also helped me put on the new self. I determined, for example, to eat at a different cafeteria than the one on the first floor of the girls' dorm. It's amazing how much lust can be eliminated by not placing yourself where six or seven hundred girls walk by your table three meals each day. I also determined to renew my mind with God's Word and began memorizing three verses a week during the following three months. At the time, I didn't understand the spiritual connection or impact, but I can still remember the day I met a very attractive girl in our ministry and realized after a delightful conversation that I had no lustful thoughts about her. God was at work, and I experienced a joy that was new to my Christian life. I put away the old, renewed my mind with the Word of God, and put on the new attitude of treating the opposite sex in my thoughts and words in ways that I knew honored God. Miraculously, refreshing friendships with sisters in Christ developed in my life. I discovered a depth and intimacy with the other half of the body of Christ that had been completely lacking as long as I held on to my old way of living. God's way truly was better. I was experiencing holy transformation in an area of my life that had been consistently marked by failure, defeat, and guilt.

Another significant step for me involved breaking

off some relationships that continually dragged me down. Bar hopping on Friday nights was simply part of my life during those first two years I was a believer. I rationalized that I didn't drink, and I was only there to help my non-Christian buddies come to Christ. But the same old thing happened Friday after Friday. I did nothing much to change them, and they did a lot to drag me down. Hanging out in bars was a habit that had to go. I made a decision, stuck with it, and replaced the old habits with some positive activities and relationships on Friday nights. Another amazing thing happened. I actually found the joy and meaning I was missing during those hours in the bars in new interactions involving positive activities helping others. This holy transformation was beginning to catch hold now, and I was seeing more clearly that doing life God's way included a whole new set of benefits. I actually sensed in my daily life what Jesus meant when He said that He came to give me life and give it to me more abundantly (John 10:10).

These were big steps for me at the time, but God was only starting His work of transformation in my life. The morphing process never ends. Three years later, in seminary, God brought about another major step of holy transformation in my life.

A MORPHING MOMENT

I remember one distinct moment during a brown-bag lunch about six years after I became a Christian. I was attending seminary, and eight or nine of us had a chance for regular meals with a godly professor, Dr.

Howard Hendricks. The meals were light, but the conversation was heavy. We talked about goals, priorities, schedules, planning, discipline—almost every "how to live life" topic you can imagine. We expressed our opinions. He let us ramble. But I will never forget the way he brought the conversation to a standstill when he finally spoke up. His words cut through like an arrow. "Look, guys," he said, glancing around to make sure he had our attention, "you've got to get this. It's grace! The Christian life from beginning to end is *grace!*" The word hung in the air, a featherweight shaft that would pierce our souls. Most of the men in that room were high-performance, driven, type A personalities, like me. Our conversation had been almost entirely about how we were going to make a great impact and do great things for God. Dr. Hendricks had us in the center of his sights when he said, "It's grace." After that, he made a statement that I will never forget as long as I live. He said,

> Look, men. There are two things you must understand:
>
> Number one—There's nothing you can do to make God love you any more than He does right now.
>
> Number two—There's nothing you can do that will cause God to love you any less than He does right now.
>
> Get this down, gentlemen. You are loved by God right where you are today as much as He will ever love you. What you do has nothing to do with how loved you are. Now, you got that?

There was something about the timing and the tone of his words that forever imprinted them in my mind.

While we were still trying to digest his words, he walked to the blackboard and wrote four terms: **Objectives, Plans, Schedule,** and **Discipline.** He said, "Men, I've been around ministries and people in the marketplace all over the world for over thirty years. Here's what I've learned. Once you understand you're fully loved—you clearly grasp that central fact that it's all by grace—you can also see that grace doesn't mean you do nothing. Grace means that based on God's great love you live a life by His power that is wholly pleasing to Him. Now, let me show you how that works."

He walked back to where he started writing, "**First, what's your objective?** If it's to be rich, that's what you'll go for. Is it to be famous? That's what you'll go for. If you want to know Christ, you need to write at the top of your list, 'I want to be a man of God.' That's your objective."

We nodded, sure we understood.

"Do you know where that'll take you?" Before any of us could volunteer an answer, he said, "Nowhere." He had us. "You've got to have a plan," he said, pointing to the second word. "How are you going to get there? **What's your plan to become a man of God?** What's it going to take? Objectives (for those who don't cheat) determine behavior. If you really want to be a man of God, you've got to develop a clear-cut plan to get there. What will it mean in terms of time in the Word of God? How will your objective determine the other books you read? In what ways will your objective determine what you choose to do or choose not to do—not because you think you have to or because you're going to gain brownie points with God, but because by His grace you want to be all that God wants you to be? What's it going to cost your gut and your heart to be a man of God?"

We gulped.

Dr. Hendricks pointed at the first term again. "There's your target, your objective. Then you have to come up with a plan that will allow you to hit the target. **Once that's in motion, you've got to make your plan a part of your schedule.**" He pointed to the third term. "Becoming a man of God becomes the first priority in your day-timer. I know many people who have a great plan to meet God every morning, but the plan doesn't mean much if it isn't put into action tomorrow morning and every morning."

We must have blinked, because he seemed to read our minds. "You don't say, 'I don't have time to meet with God.' Are you kidding me? He created everything. You start your day with Him. And then you plan in when you're going to read. And you plan in how you're going to be in a small group, and you make sure your plan includes your roles with your family. The man of God will be a man of God for his wife and kids...not just in the pulpit."

Finally, he said, "**The last one is discipline— self-control.** You discipline yourself. The difference between those who have an impact on lives and those who don't is simply that the latter group doesn't want it badly enough. Period. How badly do you want to be a man of God? Once you really understand God's grace and His unconditional love for you, the essence of living out Christianity is in the will."

He knew us so well. He almost smiled as he sliced away our superficial attitudes.

See? The real issue is we're not very honest with each other or ourselves. We say, "I want to be a man of God," but what we really mean is, "I want to be a man of God as long as it doesn't interfere with watching Sports Center, or the house I want, or one of my hobbies, or being involved in ninety-seven activities that make everybody like me." I've got news for you. Those don't go together. If you really make becoming a man or woman of God your target, that means that a whole lot of other good and bad activities will no longer even be on your radar screen. You will prioritize your life. If the target is to walk with God, you will come up with a specific plan for where you're at in your life. With some coaching and some help, you will put it in your schedule, and then the difference will be discipline. It's wanting it bad enough to stay on your schedule.

It took Dr. Hendricks less than five minutes to have his say. I've seen his words proven true in countless lives, especially my own.

I walked out of that room challenged to the core of my being. My life has never been the same. I spent a three-hour block clarifying how badly I wanted to be a man of God. There weren't big moral issues on the surface that I needed to address. In fact, my life actually looked pretty good on the outside, but there were issues in my heart that couldn't co-exist with a passionate pursuit of knowing Christ. I was brought face-to-face with a startling reality—**if I wanted to be a man of God, then I needed to reorganize my life and my heart.** Do you know what that was? I was putting on the new man. The man who went to lunch thought of himself as a man *for God*. The man who came back from lunch realized he needed to be a man *of* God. Until that lunch, I was a Christian with my own agenda. I was busy in seminary. I had big plans, but an unclear target. I was driven to get ready to serve God—the emphasis was on what I was going to accomplish for God, not what God might accomplish in me. I was much too focused on me and not nearly focused enough on God's grace. That lunch turned into a major morphing experience with God.

How about you? On your mind's screen, what do you need to bring up from the files in your mental computer and then delete? What would cause you to say, "I'm not going there anymore or acting that way anymore"? What part of the old life are you still wearing like an old shirt? When will you put it off? The Bible makes the choice clear: "Do not conform any longer to the pattern of this world, but be transformed by the renewing of your mind. Then you will be able to test and approve what God's will is—his good, pleasing and perfect will" (Romans 12:2). What would you have to do in order to start renewing your mind continuously? And what target needs to be written on the wall in your life and appear as the permanent screen-saver on your mind?

FROM SEMINARY TO DEATH ROW

Holy transformation can happen anywhere. It happened to me in seminary; it can happen to you wherever you are at this moment. I received a letter recently that highlights God's amazing ability to morph men and women into Christlikeness. God seems to do some of His best work in places we call God-forsaken. This letter came with an unusual return address and an unexpected story:

> Greetings from San Quentin State Prison—death row. I'm writing you today to voice my encouragement and support for your radio ministry Living on the Edge. I continue to catch your weekday program on KFAX and I want you to know I'm learning, growing, and applying God's Word to my life. . . .

Listen carefully to this man's story as he awaits the electric chair. Listen for the principles we've been learning about: he *takes off,* he *renews continually,* and he *puts on.* His note continues:

> I am embarking on a huge change in my walk with Christ. When I first received Christ in June of '97 I felt compelled to isolate myself from most here in prison. That's the best word—isolation—I can think of to describe how I pulled back from the world. More to the point, I isolated myself from the temptations that I wasn't yet able to resist. So I haven't been to the yard (that's where

you can go outside) every day, any day, for the first 4–5 years of my Christian life.

Until then, I was part and parcel of the convict mentality. I was out in the yard, and I did all the things we did out there.

After meeting Christ, however, I separated myself from the other prisoners. For years I've saturated myself with God's Word in various ways, and now I feel ready to face some of those old nemesises head on. I also feel that I truly need the fellowship of other believers.

For years, this formerly hardened criminal said no to an old lifestyle in the only way open to him. He isolated himself while in prison, on death row. He filled his mind for years with God's Word, breaking down old ways of thinking and renewing his perspective. Now notice what he says as he continues:

Meanwhile as I was praying this through, a body of believers had formed on another cellblock, and those brothers eventually invited me to join them. They told me they were spending three to four hours studying the Word together. That's what I was looking for—renewing and fellowship.

Now look at the "putting on" stage of this man's experience.

So I went to the powers that be to request a yard change. It turned out that was a seemingly impossible obstacle. Such a request is normally rejected outright, and they told me as much. But as the Scriptures say, "The heart of the king are as rivers in the palm of God's hands and he turns it whichever way he wishes." I simply continued on my walk of faith. My personal isolation and positive changes had become known to the powers that be and they said they would at least consider my request. They would give me their decision in a week. I accepted that whatever the outcome would be, it would be the Lord's will, and that would be fine. And then yes, they granted my request with a smile.

Now, oh happy days! Most in here only recall me as Rick of the old. They're meeting Richard of the new. I will "ease into the yard," simply put in the words of one of the powers that be. As he reviewed my file, he couldn't help but comment, "You were quite the guy out there, weren't you?" Shamefully, yes. But now I'm so excited about reaping the fellowship of other believers since I'm so desperately needy. Now I also want to contribute my own testimony and growth to the body here in prison. Why? So that maybe, just maybe, I'll be able to speak to others that are trapped in the very temptations that tripped me up and had a grip on my life for 14 years. I pray that I now might draw them to Christ. Please pray for me.

That brother in Christ is living a life of holy transformation in prison. Given who God is, there's no reason why you can't live a holy life wherever you are right now. Think of the threefold transformation that God will help you accomplish. **Take off the old. Renew your mind. Put on the new.** If you're not sure where to begin, I'd like to provide you with two sets of application questions that can help you clarify the particular ways in which God may be leading you in your journey of holy transformation.

1. In what areas of your life did God convict you personally as you thought about "putting off the old"? Where is your life not holy? In what way or ways do your thinking, actions, speech, or attitudes not reflect the new you? If you're seriously realizing, "I guess I don't have a new me because I never have trusted Jesus Christ," then why don't you pray and ask God to forgive you of your sins. Ask Him right now to come into your life, and He will.

2. What will it look like to follow God's threefold principles of transformation? Be as specific as is appropriate. Write it out.

    • I will **put off**—fill in the blank. What do you need to "put off" this week? By doing what? I will "put off _____

    _____

    _____

    • I will begin to **renew my mind by**—fill in the blank. What are you going to do? I will

begin to renew my mind by _____
_____
_____

• I will **put on**—fill in the blank. What specific behaviors has God shown you need in order to be part of the transformed life He wants you to live? What actions need to replace the old habits? I will put on _____
_____
_____

I'd like to end this chapter by praying for you. In the next few pages, we will be learning how to practically and specifically cooperate with the morphing process. People often arrive at the decision to cooperate with God's morphing process only to find yet another round of spiritual discouragement. I want to help you avoid that! But for this moment, think seriously about the areas that God's Spirit pointed out to you above. Are you ready for holy transformation?

A PRAYER OF THANKS

Lord, thank You that it is possible to be holy and whole. We confess that we can't do it on our own, but it is by Your grace through faith. That grace is the grace that teaches us to say no to worldly passions and the things that taste so good on the front end but bring havoc on the back end. We want to break free of destructive lifestyles. We want to reflect who You are and who You made us to be. Please help us deal honestly with what we need to "put off," and grant us the will and desire to systematically get into Your Word to "renew our mind." Allow us to sense Your presence and pleasure as we take specific steps to "putting on the new us" that You have made us in Christ. Amen.

11
WHY TRYING HARD TO BE HOLY DOESN'T WORK

EPHESIANS 4:25–32

M ost of what you have read in this book up to this point has been foundational. I've tried to include immediate practical application steps along the way, but the chapters have been designed to give us a fresh biblical perspective on our longing for genuine and godly transformation. I hope you have realized that your desire for deep, meaningful life-change is neither strange nor unusual. I pray that your appreciation for the way God has wired you has intensified. I also trust that you are fully committed to the idea that God is more interested in, capable of, and involved in transforming you than you could ever be.

In the last couple of chapters we have discussed the basic principles of transformation: *put off, be renewed,* and *put on.* These are vivid and timeless terms that need timely, personal, and persistent application. I asked you to be open to the places in your life that God's Spirit might be targeting for transformation. I have no way of knowing how clearly those places for change are apparent in your life, but I do know from my own experience that I need starting points. I need places in my life where I know God always wants to work. I'm convinced this is one of the reasons God inspired the apostle Paul to conclude Ephesians 4 with such practical and specific instructions about how to live a holy life. These verses are pure application. **In the sense of putting everything else we have talked about into action in your life, these last two chapters will probably be the most important,** because what we're going to talk about is the role of **spiritual training.**

What I'm about to share is one of the most neglected and misunderstood aspects of spiritual growth among Christians. And I say emphatically, if you don't get a firm grasp on the crucial role of spiritual training in your life, you will forever be frustrated in your attempts to cooperate with God's program of holy transformation. So let me start with a story with which almost all of us can identify.

SCENES FROM A LIFE UNDER TRANSFORMATION

As most parents know, our children pass through various stages in life while they are growing up. Those early teen years can be notably difficult, especially for boys. One of my sons had a particular besetting sin in his life that continually brought a painful cycle of failure, guilt, remorse, resolve to do better, and then failure yet again. What he was doing was wrong, and he knew it. He wanted to change. He tried in multiple ways to change. I had him memorize verses. I grounded him. I spent time talking and counseling with him. I explained everything I knew about Ephesians 4 that you have been reading. I told him about the importance of putting off, renewing our minds, and putting on—and yet the results were always the same. That persistent sin would raise its ugly head and in a moment of weakness my son would find himself doing the very thing he promised himself and God he would never do. During one of our many father-son talks, he burst into tears and said, "Dad, I'm sorry. I'm sorry. I'm sorry." In between his sobs, he groaned, "I'm trying, Dad. I'm trying as hard as I can! What else can I do? No matter how hard I try, I can't seem to get victory in this area!"

Something happened as I listened to my son's desperate words. A light came on inside. I suddenly realized that I had failed to teach him one of the most important lessons of spiritual transformation. After praying about the situation for a day or two, I told my son I would pick him up after school so that he and I could spend some personal time together. I also asked him to stop by the gym and put on his tennis shoes and a pair of sweatpants before he met me. When he got in the car, he still had no idea where we were going.

I have a good friend who owns a fitness center in our area, and I had already asked for permission to bring my young son in for a workout. As we walked into the impressive facilities of the World Gym, my son's eyes got big. I could tell he was puzzled about why I had brought him there. As we strolled through

the various sections of the building, we saw row after row of complicated weight machines and other
exercise equipment. The place was crowded with
bodybuilders of various ages, all sporting bulging
muscles. We watched for a moment as one athlete,
wearing a wide leather belt, bent over a bar that held
massive weight. The veins in his neck stood out and
his arms rippled with strength. As he strained to lift
the bar, it actually bowed under the weight of the
iron disks attached to each end. Sheer strength over-
came gravity and the barbell rose above the man's
head and then crashed to the mat. My son was clearly impressed; I was intimidated.

We eventually found an unoccupied bench
press, and I proceeded to introduce my son to the
object lesson that God had brought to mind as he
had shared his struggles over sin with me. He had
seen his older brothers lift weights, so he understood
the idea, but he was not ready for the lesson he was
about to learn. I had him lift some light weights to
get warmed up. Then I added just enough weight to
the bar to make it possible for him to still lift it, but
not completely. He was on his back, with his arms
extended. I stood over him, lifted the bar from its
cradle, and placed it in his outstretched hands. He
slowly lowered the bar until it touched his chest, but
when he tried to lift it back to my waiting hands, he
ran into difficulty. A few inches above his chest, the
bar stopped and his arms began to shake under the
strain. Instant beads of perspiration appeared on his
forehead and he groaned from the effort. I shouted
encouragement and exhorted him to keep pushing,

but I kept my hands above the bar. In response to my coaching he said through gritted teeth, "I'm trying, Dad. I'm trying!"

I yelled back, "Try harder, son. Try harder!"

"I'm trying, Dad," he whimpered as his arms began to wobble and the bar began to fall to his neck. Just before it did, I intervened. I lifted the bar off his chest and placed it back on the stand.

Father and son looked at each other for a moment. My son was completely exhausted. He was also confused, wondering why I was doing this to him. He slowly sat up on the bench and I joined him. "Ryan," I asked, "did you try as hard as you could to lift that bar?"

He answered, "Yes, Dad, I tried as hard as I could."

"Well," I asked, "then why didn't you lift the bar?"

"'Cause I'm not strong enough!" he admitted with a touch of anger and sadness.

"Don't you have muscles?" I asked.

"Sure, I do," he answered, "but I still couldn't lift that bar!"

We sat there in silence for a moment, surrounded by huge men who had spent countless hours developing their bodies into muscular specimens. I said, "Ryan, are you willing to agree with me, based on what we just went through, that no matter how hard you try, there are certain things you can't do by trying alone?"

He looked at me with one of those son's looks that told me he realized we were talking about more than weightlifting, but he wasn't quite sure what point I was trying to make.

I said, "Ryan, let me put it this way. Do you see these men here?" I pointed to a couple of hulks nearby.

"Yes," he murmured.

"Do you think he could lift those three hundred pounds on his bar the very first time he tried?"

"No," said Ryan.

"So, how do you think he got to the place where he can lift them as effortlessly as he's doing right now?" I asked.

Silently, Ryan watched a demonstration of strength on another weight machine for a moment, shook his head, and said to me, "Dad, I don't know."

"Ryan, it wasn't by trying hard, was it? I mean that's what we just demonstrated," I said.

He gave a little smile and nodded.

"It was by going into training, son," I continued. "If you came in here three times a week for the next six weeks and each time we raised the weight one or two pounds, do you think you would eventually be able to raise that bar off your chest?"

"Yeah, Dad, I'm sure I could," he answered.

"So, in other words, you realize that you have whatever it takes in you now, but it needs to be developed before you can accomplish your goal. You would have to go into training in order to be able to do what you cannot do right now."

He rubbed his sore arms but nodded as he said, "Yes."

"Well, listen, son," I added, "life is filled with challenges that you will never overcome by trying hard, but that you can master if you will go into training."

Sitting with my son on that weight machine bench, I saw the lights go on in his eyes. We began to talk about his besetting sin again, with a whole new perspective. Now I had a basis to explain to Ryan why he would never overcome that sin as long as his approach only involved various forms of trying harder. Holy transformation is not about trying hard. Holy transformation requires that we understand the truth we have studied in this book:

1. Every believer is called to morph—to holy transformation (Ephesians 4:1–6).
2. Christ's defeat of sin, death, and Satan makes morphing possible (Ephesians 4:7–10).
3. The church is God's primary agent of morphing in our lives (Ephesians 4:11–16).
4. We achieve personal purity (or holiness) by God's threefold principles of transformation (Ephesians 4:17–24):
   a. Put off
   b. Be renewed
   c. Put on

and finally,

5. **Transformation is a matter of spiritual training as opposed to trying harder** (Ephesians 4:25–32).

I am convinced that the majority of believers simply do not understand this last truth. I believe there are people reading this book right now who have out-of-control tempers, tongues that are untamed, private lives marked by lust, dishonesty, and a host of sins that produce cycle after cycle of failure, guilt, and defeat. I believe that many Christians are trying very, very hard but are not changing. They may even understand and agree with the first four points above. But they do not understand the role of spiritual training that produces transformation.

GOD'S TRAINING PROGRAM

In Ephesians 4:25–32, the apostle Paul, inspired by the Holy Spirit, takes the threefold principles of transformation and fleshes them out in five specific areas of spiritual training. These five areas, I believe, are given in an intentional sequence to teach you and me how genuine life-change occurs 24/7—every day of the week. These are areas we all share in common. Every one represents a specific aspect of our life in which God wants to bring about continuous progress in holy transformation. Note that Figure 11.1 provides an overview of Ephesians 4:25–32:

As you look at Figure 11.1, you see that the Holy Spirit has directed the apostle Paul to address the core issues of our lives where transformation needs to occur. Notice that unless we go into training in the area of **personal integrity** there is no hope whatsoever of personal transformation. That's where training

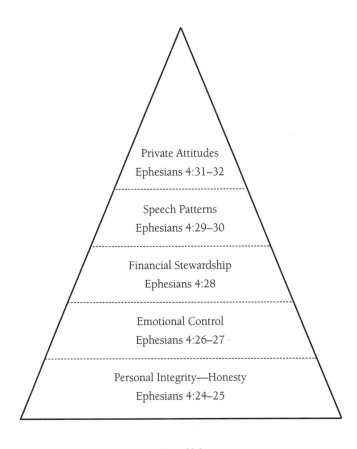

Figure 11.1

starts. What God desires most is truth in our inner-most parts. Jesus tells us the Father seeks those who worship Him in spirit and truth (John 4:24). Unless we can learn to be honest with ourselves, honest with God, and then in turn honest with others, real trans-formation will never occur. Psychologists call the op-posite of personal integrity "duplicity" or "denial." Many of us do not see transformation occurring in our lives because we do not know how to go into training in the area of personal integrity.

Once the muscles of personal integrity are strength-ened, we then move on to the next area of **emotional control.** The Bible is very clear that the anger of man does not achieve the righteousness of God (James 1:20). Most of us live lives dominated by our feel-ings. So as we study Ephesians 4:26–27 we will learn how to go into training in the area of our emotions. In the sections that follow I will walk through very specific ways to go into training in each of these areas. For the moment, I want you to see an overview of the process that God will take you through that will result in holy transformation.

Once integrity and emotional control begin to make progress under the Holy Spirit's guidance, the next arena of discipline will involve our **financial stewardship.** At the heart of stewardship is learning to work in a way that honors God. This involves not only doing things God's way but also becoming a generous person who provides for the needs of oth-ers. Jesus was emphatic and unapologetic when He stated that our heart will always follow our treasure (Matthew 6:21). Is it any wonder that the apostle

Paul gives us clear direction about how to go into training in this critical area of life?

The next level of spiritual training involves our **speech patterns.** Because the way we speak reveals the true attitudes of our hearts, here we will learn how to enter into graduate-level spiritual training that will get control of our tongues. We will discuss specific training practices that will bring your tongue under the Holy Spirit's control. But for now, I want you to see that spiritual transformation involves training in specific and strategic areas of not only the external aspects of your life, but also and more importantly the internal issues of your heart.

The highest level of spiritual training will address **private attitudes** that overflow into relationships. Deeply rooted attitudes like anger, malice, and bitterness can be transformed into forgiveness, kindness, and compassion as we enter spiritual training rather than seeking to try harder and harder to be kind and forgiving toward those who have offended us.

If this idea of spiritual training versus trying hard is still a bit foggy in your mind, let me provide another very practical example that may help you get a grasp of this fundamental principle of spiritual growth: **Some changes in our lives will never be achieved by increasing our efforts (trying harder) but only by going into spiritual training.**

HOW TRAINING WORKS

Please follow along as I describe a classic illustration I watched unfold in our church office. As we accompany this training adventure, I'll point out some of the spiritual training parallels. Not long ago, Ann, a woman in her mid-forties, decided that she wanted to run a marathon. She'd never run in her life. Another lady in our church, who is a good friend and my executive assistant Annette, is an experienced runner. She's finished many marathons. Picture, if you will now, a person who has decided she wants to run 26.2 miles without stopping. This may sound insane to you and me, or at least painful. But this woman had a goal and a desire. She wanted to change from someone who dreamed of crossing the finish line to someone who actually did it! She longed to accomplish something of significance and value that was presently impossible for her unless she went into training.

It's obvious to you and me what would have happened if she had simply said, on the day of the marathon, "I'm going to try really, really hard to run 26.2 miles without stopping even though I have never run before." She would have failed. None of us would be surprised if after less than a mile, or maybe two or three, exhaustion, severe blisters, and shortness of breath caused her to stop. This would not mean she was a bad person. Nor would it mean that her body is incapable of running a marathon distance. It wouldn't even mean she hadn't tried as hard as she could. But it would mean that she hadn't trained. Her body had in itself the capability of accomplishing her goal, but trying hard would not get her there. She would have to cooperate with what her body already possesses and take her muscles, her lungs, and her mind into training to prepare them for the task ahead. By training she could transform potential into reality. The capacity to run a marathon is within almost everyone; but most of us have never gone into training to bring our bodies to the point of doing that which is already in them.

So how does it work? Annette took this woman aside and said, "I'll help you. Everything you need to run a marathon resides in you. Your lungs are big enough, your legs are strong enough—everything you need is there. It just needs to be developed. I'll be your one-woman accountability group. I will team up with you. Now, here's what you need to understand. For the next five months we're going to go into training together." And they did.

Annette developed a systematic plan for our friend that would help her develop the strength and capacity to run 26.2 miles. Annette gave her a plan for how much sleep she would need. She went into strict training about what she could eat. There were certain activities that were now off-limits and other activities that gradually took their place in Ann's life.

They started out just jogging a little and then walking. There was a little soreness, but nothing too drastic. The jogging gradually turned into runs that covered two or three miles. About two months later, I heard them talking at the water cooler. Ann and Annette had run ten miles that Saturday morning. It sounded impossible to me, but, two months after going into training, a woman who had never run before had just run ten miles without stopping. About four months into their journey, I heard then discussing a sixteen-mile run that took most of the day. To say the least, I was in awe.

And yet, little by little, Ann brought her body into subjection to her will, preparing it to do what she wanted it to do. Her lungs expanded. Her muscles became toned and strengthened. Her will and her mind learned to overcome the pain at each mile marker. As a result of going into training, Ann was now doing what was formerly impossible for her.

About five months later, Ann (with Annette) accomplished what Ann had assumed was an impossible dream. They ran 26.2 miles. Ann didn't do it because she's stronger or better than you and me. She did it because she went into training. She didn't get up each day for a number of months and say, "I'm going to try really, really hard to run a marathon." Instead, she followed a very specific plan that allowed her to develop, over time, the capacity to do what she could not do before. It's called training.

Just as the above principles are true in the physical world, they are also true in the spiritual world. We can go into training to overcome a sharp tongue. We can train to curb lustful thoughts. We can train ourselves for acts of service or to develop a greater capacity for love. We can go into training to bring our tempers under control. The Spirit of God dwells in you and me. But the metamorphosis of your inner life is not automatic. It requires spiritual training.

I am amazed at how many Christians have so little knowledge of spiritual training. Please don't think that the concept of spiritual training is new or something that I developed. In both the Old and New Testaments we find God's people practicing spiritual training in order to live the life that He has granted us by grace. The last two thousand years of church history is filled with godly men and women who have given instruction about spiritual training so that we can become all that God has made us to be in Christ. Two books that have helped shape my thinking in this area that you might consider reading are: Dallas Willard's *The Spirit of the Disciplines*[1] and John Ortberg's *The Life You've Always Wanted.*[2] Willard's volume is thicker and a bit more complex, but a powerful and interesting read. Ortberg, in contrast, emphasizes the practical aspects of spiritual training and develops in greater detail some of the concepts we can only touch on briefly in this book.

In fact, the next and final chapter will be a beginner's manual and helpful introduction to the exciting adventure of spiritual training. I trust it will open a door of hope for you, particularly in areas where you may have struggled and tried hard for years, only to report failure. You are a perfect candidate for God's spiritual training program!

12
GOD'S SPIRITUAL TRAINING PROGRAM

EPHESIANS 4:25–32

A thletics have been a part of my life as far back as I can remember. My dad was an athlete. From the time I could pick up a ball or swing a bat, I played whatever sport was in season. I eventually competed in both basketball and baseball during college. Years later, I still show up at the gym two or three times each week, working at staying in shape. Thirty years of working out has turned into a good habit.

I'm always amazed when I see someone walk into the gym for the first time. I can sense how intimidated he must feel as the personal trainer leads him from machine to machine, explaining how each one works. The exercise "rookie" carries a clipboard with sheets that describe each exercise and the suggested number of "reps" required for maximum effect. At first the process is confusing and overwhelming. But the trainer asks about the goals and tests the current physical condition of his new client. Together, they develop an exercise program that will help that new client's body become all it was designed to be.

Back muscles must be strengthened. The upper body will require a range of stretching and strengthening exercises. Legs and abdomen will be pushed to new limits. Almost every activity will include enough repetitions and strain in order to expand cardiovascular capacity. All this and much more will be part of a fitness program that results in a body that feels, looks, and functions in a way that reflects its original design. **Getting and staying in shape isn't about trying; it's about training.**

In like manner, God has provided a very clear spiritual training program in Ephesians 4:25–32. The first twenty-four verses we've covered can be seen as an appointment with our spiritual fitness trainer, the Holy Spirit. We have learned about the goals and purposes of the kind of life God intends for us to live. Now it's time for the specific exercise plan. Instead of leading us to five weight and resistance machines to tone our biceps, triceps, and quadriceps, the Holy Spirit shows us five pivotal areas in the spiritual life that must undergo training in order for holy transformation to occur. So let's suit up and prepare to enter into God's training program for our souls.

As noted in the last chapter, there is a clear and intentional progression that affects each of the areas of spiritual training. These exercises build on one another. So I ask you to open your heart. Be sensitive to the Spirit's work as you prepare—not to *try harder* to be a better Christian but to *depend on the Spirit of*

God as you learn to appropriate God's grace and experience lasting holy transformation.

As we move into the spiritual gym, realize that God expresses each of His five training stations as a clear and emphatic command. As you reach each station, take a moment to look at the sign over the station. It will provide you with the specific objective of the exercise, the biblical command behind it, and the training actions involved. You can then refer back to these five signs as you pursue your own spiritual training. For now, take the time to read through the explanation and illustrations under each training station. These will give you some excellent starting points as you go into training for holy transformation.

SPIRITUAL TRAINING STATION 1

> Therefore each of you must put off falsehood and speak truthfully to his neighbor, for we are all members of one body.
> EPHESIANS 4:25

- ❒ **Training Objective:** Honesty (Personal Integrity)
- ❒ **Training Command:** "Speak the truth in love" (see Ephesians 4:15, 25)
- ❒ **Training Actions:**
  Put off—falsehood
  Renew—recognition of shared membership in the body
  Put on—truthful speech
- ❒ **Training Apparatus:** Practice Confession

The first training exercise involves the development of personal integrity. "Therefore each of you must *put off falsehood* and *speak truthfully* to his neighbor, for we are all members of one body" (Ephesians 4:25, emphasis added). Paul is reintroducing a command he wrote in Ephesians 4:15. Notice what's "put off"—falsehood, and what's "put on"—speak truthfully. The reason? "For we are all members of one another." Put off falsehood; put on truth. Why? Because there's a new relationship in Christ. The word *neighbor* here has the idea of fellow believers. Another translation says, "We are not separate units. But we're intimately related to one another in Christ" (PHILLIPS 1958).

Pretending, hypocrisy, saying what you don't really mean, flat-out lying—these prevent or destroy relationships. Relationships are built on trust. That means we've got to be honest with one another. That means we've got to speak the truth in love.

It's actually not too difficult to speak just the truth or to just love. The first tells people what they need to hear, but in a way that does damage because the truth is not delivered in love. The second often gives people wishy-washy responses that attempt to be loving, but fail to say the hard things that really need to be said. We need to speak the truth in love. How do we do that? Luke 16:10 presents a financial truth but it's also a timeless general principle. "He who is faithful in a very little thing is faithful also in much; and he who is unrighteous in a very little thing is unrighteous also in much" (NASB).

Start with the Little Things

So, how do you go into training to become an honest person? I encourage you start with the little things—for example, the little exaggerations. How many times have you found yourself driving to an appointment and traffic was a little bit slow—but you started ten minutes late and you're late for that meeting. So you just say, "Oh, the traffic was really heavy. Sorry I'm late." That's a lie. It's only part of the truth. The truth is you left ten minutes late and you don't want to own that part of it.

I had a problem with this early in my ministry. I developed a pattern of exaggerating in the little things. I just thought it was "rounding." That's what I called it. My wife didn't even call it exaggeration. She just called it lying. I'll never forget coming home after one Sunday sermon and she said, "Well, Chip, why did you lie this morning?" Now understand, my wife is a gentle, loving, kind, and warm person, but when it comes to issues of integrity, she's absolutely uncompromising! She's very direct (and I love her for it).

I said, "What do you mean?

She answered, "You said there were sixty-eight or seventy people last week at the Wednesday night service. Yet I saw you count them up and there were sixty-four."

I said, "I just rounded."

She said, "How do you round from sixty-four to sixty-eight? And why does it matter?"

I shrugged, "Well, it doesn't."

She cleverly returned to her first question, "So, why did you lie?"

The next week I gave an illustration, and on the way home she said, "Well, Chip, that was a good story and it fit your point, but it's not really what happened. Don't you remember it was our other son who said that and . . ."

Exasperated, I said, "Honey, are you going to do this every week?"

She smiled at me so sweetly as she murmured, "No—only when you lie."

We chuckle over these conversations now, but they represented a point of real tension in our marriage until I realized there were deeper issues behind my "exaggerations." God wanted me to learn to be absolutely honest even in the small stuff.

Training Apparatus: Practicing Confession

Unfortunately, many Christians have developed patterns of dishonesty that seem harmless but become the roots of denial, rationalization, compromise, and self-delusion. Going into training means eliminating little lies, white lies, or partial truths. It means that little by little you make progress. You start telling the truth in love.

Over the years, I've discovered a tool that I've found helpful. I call it **practicing confession.** I've learned that this painful exercise curbs my tendency to bend the truth. Practicing confession means that every time I lie, whether it's little or big, I go back and tell the person I've lied unless it would harm someone to tell. This has really helped me develop integrity in my life. I made a commitment to **practice confession** and have been training in this area for more than twenty years. I've seen real improvement, but the way hasn't always been easy.

Some seventeen years ago, a representative from a major mission organization was putting a basketball team together to travel, play, and minister in China. China was a closed country. He'd already invited a good seminary friend who was 6'11" and a great ballplayer. We were on an intramural team together. Then he called me. What an opportunity!

When he asked me how I was doing in basketball I said, "Oh, I'm in the best shape ever."

He asked, "How many points are you averaging?"

Well, the league didn't keep track of stats, so I "rounded." "You know, Bud, probably twelve to fourteen points a game. Our front line goes 6'11", 6'10", 6'9"—all major college players who are on the team with me, so I'm averaging about eight or nine assists, and three or four steals a game. I'm really having a good year." Once the stats started flowing, I couldn't help myself. I mean I was trying to get on this China team.

He said, "Thanks, Chip, we're making up our squad. I'll call you back in about a week."

I hung up the phone, and the peace in my heart was gone. Now, did I know how many points I was averaging? No, we didn't have a book. Did I know how many assists? No. Was it true that I was playing alongside some excellent big players and having a good year? Yes. But do you know what I had done? I had lied. And then the Spirit of God convicted me. I could almost hear Him whisper, "You need to call Bud Schafer, the director of Sports Ambassadors, and tell him you lied."

Instead, I prayed. "But God, I'm a seminary student. I'm preparing for ministry. He's a real influential guy. Besides, this will be very humbling, and I really don't want to go there."

God didn't have to say anything. This was not a negotiation. Plan B—I told God I was very sorry and asked Him to forgive me, thinking that would be good enough. I put off calling Bud back for a day or two in hopes that the Spirit of God would make the conviction go away. Instead it got worse.

So I called Bud. I said, "Hi, Bud, this is Chip. I need to tell you something."

He said, "What's up?"

I said, "I lied . . . You know all those statistics? We don't really keep them. I made mine up. I just really wanted to be on the team. I'm embarrassed. But I've made a commitment as part of my spiritual training. I want to be an honest person. So I'm asking you to forgive me for having lied."

Knowing you will have to go back and apologize will help you begin to tell the truth in little things and in big things. And as you do, you will experience what Jesus promised—you will know the truth and the truth will set you free. This is for your good. People will begin to trust you more deeply. You won't have to remember to whom you told what. Integrity that grows from the inside out will make you a winsome and beautiful person.

As you regularly visit Spiritual Training Station 1

you will discover that little by little, rather than feeling like a failure, you will break the cycles of dishonesty by telling the truth the first time. You will eliminate those painful times of having to correct a lie and will stick more and more to the truth in every situation. Just like that woman in the last chapter who trained to run 26.2 miles, you can learn over time, by God's grace, to tell the truth to yourself, to God, and to others. This is the starting point to spiritual fitness and holy transformation.

Spiritual Training Station 2

> "In your anger do not sin." Do not let the sun go down while you are still angry, and do not give the devil a foothold.
>
> EPHESIANS 4:26–27

- ☐ **Training Objective:** Emotional Control
- ☐ **Training Command:** "Be angry, and yet do not sin" (Ephesians 4:26 NASB)
- ☐ **Training Actions:**
  Put off—anger that leads to offense and sin
  Renew—recognition of dangers in retaining anger
  Put on—appropriate expressions of anger
- ☐ **Training Apparatus:** "I feel" Messages

The second training station involves the area of anger. Spiritual growth is often thwarted by our emotional life not being controlled by the Spirit of God. In fact, the Bible points out that "the anger of

man does not achieve the righteousness of God"
(James 1:20 NASB). Yet the command in Ephesians
4:26 admits that sometimes, we need to "be angry."
Sounds wild doesn't it? Here's the key—not all anger
is a sin. Anger in and of itself is not inherently evil.
It's what we do with our anger that makes all the difference in the world. We need to learn to deal appropriately with anger. Notice the *put off/put on* and
the *why* again. "*Be angry* (put on), and yet *do not sin*
(put off); do not let the sun go down on your anger"
(Ephesians 4:26 NASB, emphasis added). Put sin off.
Why? Because staying angry gives "the devil an opportunity" (Ephesians 4:27 NASB). Or, "If you're angry, be sure that it's not out of wounded pride or a
bad temper. Never go to bed angry—don't give the
devil that sort of foothold" (4:26 PHILLIPS 1958). So
you put on appropriate anger, but you put off sinful
anger. There are times when you ought to be angry.
In fact this is a positive command. *Be angry.* When
someone cheats you, when someone robs you, when
people are unfairly hurt we should be righteously angry, but we maintain emotional control even as we
express our anger in appropriate ways.

On the dark side of anger, too many husbands
and wives go to bed mad at each other. They literally
violate this verse. He's angry because she was un-
responsive; she's angry because he won't communicate. He blows up. She withdraws. The average affair
and most break-ups in marriages don't occur because someone wakes up one day and says, "You
know something? Today's a great day for an affair. I
think I'll just walk away from all that really matters

in my life—my spouse, my children, my commitments, and my God. Yesterday was fine; today I'll wreck my marriage." We all know that's not how it happens! You know how it starts? Unresolved anger, usually. The accumulation of hurt feelings, causing withdrawal and isolation, can become a permanent condition. Anger turns into a way of seeing. You develop anger-vision. Whatever your spouse does, if 5 percent of it can be criticized, we bump it up to 20 or 25 percent negative. Even when he or she does what is right we can allow it to become a reason for anger because we think, "There, that proves they know what they should have been doing all along." If we keep the anger smoldering, we eventually drift out of our most important relationships.

Unresolved anger hardens your heart. Ephesians 4:26–27 is one of the few passages in all of Scripture that tells us how demonic activity enters relationships—go to bed with unresolved anger. You see, anger doesn't dissipate by blaming or denial. Anger recedes when we state the truth, owning our part in the problem. "The way I treated you was wrong, and I'm sorry. Please forgive me for the way I responded. I didn't listen. I acted defensively instead of helping you tackle a real problem. Will you forgive me?" And you need to get that right before you go to bed. Otherwise, when you wake up it may not seem like such a big deal. But sleeping on anger doesn't solve it. Anger lives on, down deep. It accumulates out of sight, hardening your heart.

TRAINING APPARATUS: "I FEEL" MESSAGES

Unfortunately, most of us didn't learn how to resolve anger while we were growing up. I know I didn't. But through some difficult times in this area I've discovered a tool that is very effective in resolving anger. You want to learn to become a person who has your emotions under God's control? You need to learn to deal with anger appropriately. The tool is called **"I feel" Messages.** The first five years of our marriage, my wife and I had a very difficult time resolving our anger. We weren't yellers, screamers, throwers, or blow uppers. I would get really mad and she would withdraw—it wasn't any fun after that. She wouldn't talk to me for a day or two, and then I'd try to punish her in passive-aggressive ways for a day or two. Then she would realize it wasn't really worth it, and I'd realize it wasn't worth it. We never really dealt with anger or the causes. We'd say, "OK, I'm sorry" to each other, without naming the problem. We would kiss, make up, and go on until the next time it happened, only worse.

We had a pattern. In fact, we were in *negative training.* I was building up a lot of destructive feelings inside and she was as well. Those feelings affected multiple areas in our relationship. So we went and got some marriage counseling, which, by the way, when you're having trouble in a marriage is money well spent. Our counselor said, "I've looked at your family backgrounds. You two don't know how to deal with anger, do you?" We looked at each other and then sheepishly nodded. He went on, "Let me give you a suggestion." As he wrote it on a 3 x 5 card, he said, "You two are constantly sending 'you ought' or 'you should' messages to one another when you get angry. That's only effective in making the other person defensive. You've developed a vicious cycle of communication that attacks the person instead of the problem. What you need to do is get anger on neutral ground where you share your feelings instead of attacking the other person. Where you can deal with the issue instead of with the emotion." He handed us the 3 x 5 card on which he had written:

- I feel angry when you . . .
- I feel hurt when you . . .
- I feel isolated . . . I feel left out when you . . .

He instructed us to post the card on our refrigerator and use the statements to express our feelings when we became angry.

We got to test the plan within days. I came home late—again. I was frequently late because I wanted to do "one more thing." I was always overextended. Invariably, when I did that Theresa would have cooked a great meal and be rightly upset when I had failed to return home when I promised. That usually led to a confrontation followed by defensiveness, denial, and excuses, leading up to an argument. On this particular night, however, she met me with a calm smile and then reheated supper. No hands on the hips, no "You ought" and no "You should." I thought, *Hey, maybe I dodged a bullet this time.* As I ate, Theresa sat quietly. At first, her response threw me off balance. I was fully aware that I had once again created the makings of an argument. Instead, she let me finish my meal, and then she said, quietly and deliberately, **"Chip, I really feel hurt and like maybe you don't love me when I spend this much time cooking a meal and you come home forty-five minutes or an hour late and don't even call."**

Busted. How do you argue with a feeling? I wasn't prepared for this! Her calmly stated feelings and facts dropped a load of responsibility on my head but without attacking me. I just wanted to say, "Would you just get up and fight like a man? Let's argue like before—at least I can hope for an angry tie!" Instead, she got to resolve her anger by clearly stating her feelings. I had to take responsibility for my actions. You will be amazed as you will start using "I feel" messages. Not only will they help resolve anger, they will also be good training in speaking the truth in love. For example:

- "I feel rejected when before I leave for work I want to give you a kiss and you turn the other way and get involved with the kids. It makes me feel like they're more important than me."

- "I feel hurt and lonely when you come home from work and our kids really need some attention and you watch the news, read the paper, and leave the chaos for me."

You know what the average family does? They don't say anything. Or they attack. They internalize the feelings or they blow up. You know what? It's not that hard to say, "I feel ___." Make your 3 x 5 card with suggested "I feel" statements and put it on the refrigerator.

| Anger Resolution Exercise |

I feel _____

when you _____

I would encourage you go into training in the area of anger management. Your lack of patience, emotional fallout, problems in relationships—these are areas of training for life's marathon. Make the decision "I'm going into training. I'm going to practice honesty. I'm going to become a person whose emotional lifestyle is under control."

SPIRITUAL TRAINING STATION 3

> He who has been stealing must steal no longer, but must work, doing something useful with his own hands, that he may have something to share with those in need.
>
> EPHESIANS 4:28

- ❏ **Training Objective:** Financial Stewardship (Work Ethic)
- ❏ **Training Command:** "Steal no longer" (Ephesians 4:28)

❐ **Training Actions:**
Put off—stealing
Renew—think differently about the value of work
Put on—work

❐ **Training Apparatus:** Good Mentors

The third training station involves diligence. Work hard and refuse to take shortcuts. Notice what you put off. "He who steals must steal no longer" (Ephesians 4:28 NASB). The text literally says "stop stealing." What do you put on? "But rather he must labor [work], performing with his own hands what is good" (4:28 NASB). Then get your mind renewed. Think differently about work. Look at the way Paul expresses this: "So that he will have something to share with one who has need" (4:28 NASB). Most of us have grown up with the following idea about work: *Go in as late as possible, come home as early as possible, get as little done as possible, get paid as much as possible—that's a good day's work.* Unless you own the company. Then it's *Go in before dawn and never come home, because work is all there is.*

The grammar of this verse literally is stop stealing. It's not hypothetical. There were people in this church who were stealing. He said, "*Stop stealing.* You can't do that anymore. Start laboring." The purpose of work isn't just so your needs get met. Holy transformation means that Christ is living out His life as though He were in your body. Therefore, we understand that He would work with the needs of others in mind. Unfortunately, that is not how our world tends to view work. The attitude in the world is *Find a shortcut.* You want wealth? Find a shortcut—we're infected with shortcutitis. We all seem to want the product without the pain or the process. We see it everywhere. It's the lotto ticket mentality. We live in a world of get-rich-quick schemes and infomercial miracles. Like I said, shortcutitis.

Refuse the shortcut mentality. It infects all of life. It makes us think we can live holy lives without holy training. We want to skip the hard work, we want to skip going into training, we want to skip the workouts, we want to skip going out and talking with our mate, we want to skip getting in a growth group, we want to skip daily time in the Bible, we want to skip the time it takes to learn how to pray. But we say we want to be Christlike. We want great relationships. We want a secure home. I've got news for you. Things that grow well and last grow slowly. Oak trees take a long time to grow. Weeds come up quickly. We want things to grow as fast as weeds and look like oak trees. We want to sign up for a marathon one day and win it the next.

Paul is telling us go into training in the area of diligence. How? Our primary training instrument is a new attitude toward work found in Colossians 3:23–24, "Whatever you do, work at it with all your heart, as working for the Lord, not for men, since you know that you will receive an inheritance from the Lord as a reward. It is the Lord Christ you are serving."

You see, every moment of each day becomes an opportunity to turn the monotony of the daily grind into multiple moments of personal worship. Every act—when you change a baby's diapers, when you wash the dishes, when you vacuum, when you wash the car, when you do the grass, when you go to where you work—every aspect of life can be an act of worship. Whatever you do, do it as unto the Lord. It has value because of who is receiving it. That automatically keeps us from cutting corners. God will meet us in the mundane of our everyday work. We want this big pizzazz experience that we think is going to make everything great. But as Oswald Chambers so aptly puts it, "The secret of a Christian is that the supernatural is made natural in him by the grace of God, and the experience of this works out in the practical details of life, not in times of communion with God."[1]

The people who are godly have experienced holy transformation through spiritual training, not shortcuts. It requires a rearrangement of our lives and priorities. The practice of spiritual disciplines like Bible study, prayer, and meditation never come about through shortcuts. They all require training in diligence.

One last caution on diligence. I see many believers practicing diligence without a clear sense of biblical priorities. We can easily end up being diligent in sincere but misguided directions. A change in priorities often must begin by asking ourselves some very penetrating questions. Who said your kids have to be in four youth sports? Who said your calendar has to be so full that most time slots are double-booked? Who said you have to make as much money as you make?

Even a casual look at the average American family reveals a pace and a level of busyness that makes it almost impossible for spiritual training or meaningful relationships to occur. We're pushed, busy, and diligent pursuing the American Dream rather than God's dream for our lives and our children.

Life in American culture is busyness and over-extension. We live under *pressure* instead of under *priorities*. You don't have to live that way. That's the world telling you, "Speed, speed, speed, complexity, complexity, complexity, shortcuts, shortcuts, and more shortcuts." You know what those attitudes produce? Shallowness, shallowness, shallowness.

Training in godly diligence leads to an amazing depth of life called holy transformation.

TRAINING APPARATUS: GOOD MENTORS

When it comes to the area of diligence, the value of good models needs to be emphasized. In fact, noting how other healthy Christians "work out" on each apparatus of spiritual training can often provide us with the encouragement and direction we need. As I mentioned in chapter 11, two books that have helped shape my thinking in this area and proved invaluable are Dallas Willard's *The Spirit of the Disciplines* and John Ortberg's *The Life You've Always Wanted*. These two men of God, along with others who are further down the road spiritually than we, represent the kind of good mentors we all need as we train toward holy transformation.

Spiritual Training Station 4

> Do not let any unwholesome talk come out of your
> mouths, but only what is helpful for building others
> up according to their needs, that it may benefit
> those who listen. And do not grieve the Holy Spirit
> of God, with whom you were sealed for the day of
> redemption.
>
> EPHESIANS 4:29–30

- ☐ **Training Objective:** Positive Speech
- ☐ **Training Command:** "Say only what helps"
  (the message of Ephesians 4:29)
- ☐ **Training Actions:**
  Put off—negative speech
  Renew—give grace to others and avoid griev-
  ing the Holy Spirit
  Put on—positive, encouraging speech
- ☐ **Training apparatus:** Practicing Silence and
  Solitude

The fourth training station involves your tongue.
Don't wound with your words. Paul wrote, "Do not
let any unwholesome talk come out of your mouths,
but only what is helpful for building others up according to their needs, that it may benefit those who
listen" (Ephesians 4:29). Put off "unwholesome talk"
and put on "what is helpful for building others up."
Why? Two reasons. "That it will give grace to those
who hear" (Ephesians 4:29 NASB)—that you do good
things, say positive, enriching statements in relationships. The second reason comes in the next

verse, "And do not grieve the Holy Spirit of God, with whom you were sealed for the day of redemption" (Ephesians 4:30). Or, as Phillips has it, "Never hurt the Holy Spirit. He is . . . the personal pledge of your eventual full redemption." Notice that the way we talk to others can grieve the Holy Spirit. God isn't like the Force. He is personal. He has feelings. It breaks God's heart when something comes out of our mouth that reduces another person. But each of us has known the joy of someone's coming alongside us with an encouraging word that propelled us to heights of accomplishment—we were built up.

RECOGNIZE THE POWER OF WORDS

So, how do you bring your tongue under the control of the Holy Spirit? How do you get to where, instead of speaking negative, critical, and sarcastic put-downs into people's lives, you become a source of life? First, recognize the power of words. The Scriptures say there is life and death in the power of words (see Proverbs 18:21). What comes out of your mouth literally has the power to make or break a person's day—or ruin his life. Especially if that person is younger. Especially if that person looks up to you. Especially if you are married to that person.

Luke 6:45 says that even beyond the power of words, **"The good man out of the good treasure of his heart brings forth what is good; and the evil man out of the evil treasure brings forth what is evil; for his mouth speaks from that which fills his heart"** (NASB). If you really want to know the condition of your heart before God, the place to look is not at your schedule of religious activities or even your external morality. Listen, instead, to the kind of words and the tones of voice that come out of your mouth. According to Jesus, that is the clearest indication of where your heart is with Him.

"We all make many mistakes, but those who control their tongues can also control themselves in every other way" (James 3:2 NLT). Examine your speech. James teaches us that bringing our tongues under the Holy Spirit's control represents one of the most important areas of training toward holy transformation. In essence, he says that if you and I can learn to control what comes out of our mouths, we will be able to bring our entire lives under the Spirit's reign. If that sounds like an overstatement regarding the importance of positive speech, listen to Jesus' words in Matthew 12:36, **"But I tell you that men will have to give account on the day of judgment for every careless word they have spoken."** I don't know about you, but those words send chills down my spine. How many times am I sarcastic or flippant in my speech? How many times do I say something with a harsh tone in my voice because I've had a hard day, causing my teenage daughter grief? She doesn't deserve that. Jesus warns me that I'll have to account for such thoughtless comments. I must recognize the power of words.

TRAINING APPARATUS:
PRACTICE SILENCE AND SOLITUDE

So, how can we ever gain control of this thing inside our mouths that can bring life or death to relationships? The answer is the second aspect of training for positive speech. It's almost unheard of in our day: **Learn to practice silence and solitude.** Try talking less. Proverbs tells us, "When there are many words, transgression is unavoidable" (Proverbs 10:19 NASB). That one hits me where I live. Can you imagine how much someone with a job like mine talks? My family has made me aware of it on multiple occasions. "Dad, you're not preaching. Lighten up!"

It may sound strange that someone who teaches God's Word has such struggles in this area, but I've been engaged in a very long training process (with miles to go) concerning this challenge to bring my tongue under God's control. But I'd like to share with you a practice that has helped me the most over the years.

1. **Memorize James 1:19b–20,** which says, "But everyone must be quick to hear, slow to speak and slow to anger; for the anger of man does not achieve the righteousness of God" (NASB). Having this truth in my heart has helped me bite my tongue and keep my mouth shut when I was sorely tempted to speak inappropriately.
2. **Consider journaling** at least three or four times a week in a quiet place, alone. After sitting silently before God for a while, ask Him

to show you what's been coming out of your mouth in the last day or two. Face the question, "Why?" As I write out my thoughts and examine my motives, I begin to see insecurities, fears, anxiety, and desires to impress others that have caused me to say hurtful words. Real growth has occurred during these times of solitude as God has helped me examine my speech patterns.

3. **Consider a one- or two-day personal retreat** every four to eight weeks. During personal retreats I'm not usually preparing messages or doing ministry-related work. I slow my life-pace. I walk, think, journal, pray, and rest. As I do, God is faithful to reveal junk that has come out of my mouth that I forgot about. It's like playing a little videotape. And I deal with them and I tell Him I'm sorry. When appropriate, I go back to people whom I have offended to apologize. If I keep account of my words and take care of them, I know I won't have to give an account to my heavenly Father for an out-of-control mouth.

SPIRITUAL TRAINING STATION 5

Get rid of all bitterness, rage and anger, brawling and slander, along with every form of malice. Be kind and compassionate to one another, forgiving each other, just as in Christ God forgave you.
EPHESIANS 4:31–32

❐ **Training Objective:** Holy Private Attitudes
❐ **Training Command:** "Be kind to one another, tender-hearted, forgiving each other" (Ephesians 4:32 NASB)
❐ **Training Actions:**
Put off—hate
Renew—new attitudes based on what God has done
Put on—love
❐ **Training Apparatus:** The Matthew 5:24 Principle

The fifth training station has to do with forgiveness. Be the first to say, "I'm sorry, I was wrong." The "putting-off" actions involve six different attitudes that Paul lists in Ephesians 4:31: "Get rid of all *bitterness, rage* and *anger, brawling* and *slander,* along with every form of *malice*" (emphasis mine). *Bitterness* refers to the deep-seated resentments people have toward one another. *Rage* (or wrath) is the blow-up kind of anger. The word *anger* in that verse describes a resentment and negativity that permeates all of life. *Brawling* (or clamor) refers to the kind of shouting and baiting that incites violence. *Slander* involves stealth-anger, as when you defame another person's character and say things that aren't true about him. Paul's last word, *malice,* points to the evil intent that lies behind the other five actions. Training in holiness relentlessly gets these kinds of attitudes out of your life.

Ephesians 4:32 lists the three replacement attitudes —what you put on through training: "Be *kind* and *compassionate* to one another, *forgiving* each other, just as in Christ God forgave you" (emphasis mine). *Kindness* covers a multitude of things. Kindness practices treating others "in kind" or "in the same kind of way that you want to be treated." *Compassionate* (or tenderhearted) translates the Greek word *splanchna.* It was used by and about Jesus to describe a response to other people "from the bowels," or as we would say today, a "gut-level" care for others. Compassion involves a down-deep-inside love that reaches out and meets needs. And then notice the pinnacle of being like Jesus: *forgiving each other.* That's the positive side of training. But also notice how our mind needs to be renewed. In the world's system, you hurt me and I hurt you back. If I hurt you back and you did something bad to me you deserve it. I hope it breaks you. But that's not God's system, is it? Kindness trains me to treat others as I want to be treated. Compassion shapes my responses to treat others as Jesus would treat them. And forgiveness means I learn to release others from what they justly deserve for hurting me, just as Jesus has released and forgiven me.

I don't know about you, but left to myself I want justice 100 percent of the time for everyone but me. When someone cuts me off in traffic, my flesh hopes he gets a flat tire. When someone uses me financially, I hope he goes broke. When someone is mean to me emotionally, my carnal response is to wish that bad things would happen to him. When it comes to what others do to us, we all tend to want an eye for an eye. But when I do some of the same bad behaviors, I want to be able to go to God and say, "O God, I did it again. I'm sorry. I never should have said this or done that. Will You be merciful? Can we cut a deal?" Do you know what God says? "We already cut a deal, Chip. My Son died for you. Your sinful behavior didn't surprise Me. Your lustful thoughts didn't surprise Me. Your selfishness didn't surprise Me. What came out of your mouth may have shocked you, but I've seen it in your heart. When My Son Jesus died on the cross, He paid for that. He paid for it all. Now, Chip, I want you to forgive the same way." *Holy transformation means you go into training to be a marathon forgiver.*

I have found the Matthew 5:24 principle to be an effective and practical training exercise when it comes to my private attitudes. It's where Jesus said (paraphrased), "When you come to worship God and you suddenly remember that your brother has something against you—not that you have something against him—leave your offering there until you take care of something even more important." In other words, "Put your act of worship on hold until you go to your brother and become reconciled." Our human nature, however, usually takes just the opposite approach to solving relational conflict. We tend to think about it this way: *We had a big fight—there's a real problem. Someone did something terrible, and I responded in a bad way. Now I feel guilty. Ninety percent of the problem is theirs, right? And 10 percent is my ungodly, negative response.* So we conclude, *That person is wrong, and when they come and apologize we'll get this relationship back together!* Right?

God says that the relationship is more important

than figuring out who owns what percentage of blame. When you know there's a problem with a person, God says, "Forget trying to figure out who's most responsible. **Take responsibility for your part, where you're wrong, and go to that person.**" Even if you're convinced it's 90 percent his fault, you say, "You know, Bob, we had that interchange the other day and I said some harsh things. God helped me realize I responded the wrong way, and I ask you to forgive me for how I spoke to you." You know what that usually produces? The other person often says, "Well, since you're owning that, I admit I did this." But whether he does or not isn't as important as your obedience to Christ and training in being like Him.

You say, "Chip, that's not fair!"

Of course it's not fair. Just like it wasn't fair when Jesus unilaterally forgave you for all your sin. I'm not asking you for fairness. I'm asking you to allow Jesus to live His life inside you so people get treated the way He would treat them if He were inside your body. The result is an amazing process called *holy transformation* where little by little, as in training for a marathon, you go into spiritual training to become like Christ. As you commit yourself to go into training in these five Training Stations outlined in Ephesians 4, you gradually undergo metamorphosis. God will bring about change in your heart, mind, and relationships. **This side of eternity you will never be perfect, but significant, radical life-change will be the norm in your life.**

Eventually, you will be the kind of person of

whom others say, "Someday, when I grow up I want to be like (<u>your name</u>)." As a man in my forties, I serve with men in my church who are godly models for me and who have known and walked with God longer and more intimately than I. When I pray, I often say, "God, someday I want to be like them." I sit in elders' meetings with some of them. Others I've just gotten to know and have realized that someday I want to have a marriage like theirs. I've been working at mine for twenty-four years; but they've been in training for twice that long or more—and it shows. Someday I want to have self-control like theirs. They inspire me to stay in training.

COMMITMENTS

God has a lot at stake in our training. His commitment to forgiving us cost Him the life of His own Son. He has pledged Himself to participate in every step of our transformation to become people who look and act like Jesus. His verbal commitment bears repeating. "Being confident of this, that he who began a good work in you will carry it on to completion until the day of Christ Jesus" (Philippians 1:6). God will do His part. He will be our number one training partner, coach, and cheerleader.

Our part is to appropriate His grace and power as we go into training in the areas of *personal integrity* (honesty), *emotional control* (anger), *financial stewardship* (diligence), *positive speech* (words), and *private attitudes.* So let me ask you, in which of these five areas have you made genuine progress as a believer? Sometimes we focus too quickly on the negative.

Look where you've made progress because that will give you some real help in realizing, "Hey! There's hope." Remember what Paul told Timothy when he spelled out a similar training program for his young disciple? "Be diligent in these matters; give yourself wholly to them, so that everyone may see your progress" (1 Timothy 4:15). When others know you're in training, they will notice your progress!

Now comes the tough question. *Which one of those five areas, not all five of them, do you need to go into training in order to allow the life of Christ to be lived out in a winsome, holy, and loving way in you? How will you begin that training?*

At one point in my life I realized I had a pattern of being overextended—busy beyond healthiness. As I began thinking and praying about a training plan for that concern, I realized that behind my hyper-activity was some warped and even sinful thinking. My attitude was rooted in a very subtle form of arrogance called grandiosity. I thought I was indispensable, so I had to be everywhere all the time to meet everybody's needs. Behind my inability to say no I found a huge case of pride caused by a desire to have everyone like me. I wanted to come through for everybody all the time. So I had an insane schedule. And, because I really love God and love my wife and my kids, I put them in my schedule. That meant I had ungodly hours of getting up in the wee hours of the morning and staying up too late at night.

This was an area of continual concern, but several years ago I decided to stop telling everyone that "I was going to try to slow down" and instead go into training. I wrote out some flash cards to keep me on a training regimen that set boundaries on my work and inserted times to consistently enjoy life. I play golf almost every week, nine holes. I listen to music just for fun almost every week. I schedule goof-off time. I go on a date every week with my wife, just to have fun. I've realized the work hard–compulsive side of my life is overdeveloped. Jesus isn't one-dimensional, and those who are becoming like Him aren't one-dimensional people either.

So, what does God want to develop in your heart? Maybe it's training in how to celebrate and to worship with greater freedom and joy. And maybe your training ought to be listening to some worship tapes and just singing along in the car. ***Training* is not a negative word. It's how do you arrange your life priorities and activities to become the person you long to become.** A lot of it can really be fun. In fact, this is one of the early signs that training in holiness is having an effect in your life. Things that used to be hard and not fun will begin to take on a joy that you will find amazing. What used to feel like painful and awkward flexing of wet wings will begin to feel like flight. You may not be able to put your finger on the exact day when you crossed the line between training and actually doing—but someday, under God's training, someone will pull you aside and say, "I've been watching you. What's going on? Something's happened to you—it's like, you've been transformed." Be sure to smile and whisper a prayer of thanks to the transforming Holy Spirit before you give the person a reason for the hope he has noticed in you!

CONCLUSION

Some friends of mine live in the Midwest, where the wife teaches fifth grade in a rural public school. August in Wisconsin takes on a lush, tropical quality. The rolling cornfields have reached their zenith and the tassels have done their pollinating work. Soon the stalks will turn brown and the harvest will begin. Life seems to be part of the air. As much as I love California, I sometimes miss the seasonal morphing that each year produces in other parts of the country.

In open fields and on thousands of miles of roadside, another crop reaches maturity. The broad, velvety leaves of the milkweed flourish in the sun and humidity. Break off a leaf from one of these plants and a thick, milky substance pours from the injury. It has the same consistency as white glue. Apparently, monarch butterfly caterpillars think the stuff is nectar. Here and there, healthy milkweed plants take on a ragged look overnight as ravenous caterpillars feed themselves in a frenzy of pre-metamorphosis hunger.

Summer's hiatus signals my friend's wife that the school doors will soon open. The abundance of milkweed and the monarch butterfly caterpillars that call Wisconsin home offer her a yearly start at provoking her students' curiosity about learning. She wants them fascinated about life. She collects several specimens and provides plenty of milkweed leaves until the caterpillar moves through the agonizingly slow stages of metamorphosis. The kids are drawn into the daily watch. Each caterpillar has its own quart jar complete with a cocoon stick. Each phase of metamorphosis is noted, discussed, and marveled over by the students. By the time the butterfly emerges, the entire class has usually established a connection with the creature. Usually a name gets chosen. This past year, a flight ceremony developed. When the monarch began flexing its wings for pre-take-off the entire class walked out carrying Bob (the monarch's name) perched on the stick from which his cocoon had dangled. They formed a large circle and the stick was passed from student to student, each one hoping she or he would be the one holding it when Bob took flight. The spontaneous eruption of cheering when Bob launched himself was delightful. Those kids watched Bob go from worm to wonder! Who's watching the changes in your life?

I can't see what God's been doing in you as you have read these chapters, but I am absolutely convinced He wants to create holy transformation in you. If you have placed your faith in Jesus Christ, I remind you that you are no longer a caterpillar but a beautiful butterfly. The principles spelled out in Ephesians 4 are the spiritual foundation for God changing you and changing me. Let's look at them one more time.

- **We began by learning that every believer is called to morph.** In other words, transformation, life change, becoming a loving, pure, holy, winsome person. It's not for superstars. It's for every believer, including you.

- **Then we learned that Christ's defeat of sin, death, and Satan makes morphing possible.** The power exercised in Christ's death and His resurrection is available to make a difference in our lives. This isn't about pulling yourself up by your bootstraps. This isn't about trying harder. There was a spiritual event that occurred when the Son of God, fully man and fully God, died and was resurrected. He defeated the power of sin, death, and the Enemy. It's in his power. Your identity in Him is the basis for all change.

- **Next we learned that the church—and I don't mean the church building, but the church, God's people connected to one another—is God's primary agent of morphing in our lives.** He's going to use other people rooted in the Word of God and empowered by His Spirit to help you discern and deploy your spiritual gifts for the common good. As you get connected, you're going to rub up next to people. Leaders are going to lead and saints are going to be equipped. People will exercise gifts and exude joy. As all that happens, a supernatural synergy will occur. That's how life-change happens.

- **Then we learned we achieve personal holiness, that winsome loving moral purity, by God's threefold process of transformation.** Remember the three steps? First, put off—get your old cocoon-life behind you. Second, have your mind be transformed. And third, put on the new life in Christ. Remember Paul's metaphor of clothes? It was a picture of a shabby, useless jacket—your old life. Taking it off in a point in time, focusing and renewing your mind on what's true, and putting on the new self. Becoming like Christ.

- **Finally, we learned that transformation is a matter of spiritual training as opposed to trying harder.**

In the last two chapters we looked at the five specific areas, given in ascending order, to train you and me in how genuine life change becomes ours. God has provided everything we need to live morphed, holy, and winsome lives.

Those fifth-grade students who cheered as Bob the butterfly took flight on that brisk fall day represent the unseen crowd cheering your progress toward holy transformation. Many of them you will not see this side of eternity, but they are pulling for you. They will be thrilled to see you engaging in the kind of training that leads to spiritual morphing. They will shout over every new step. They are living proof that it can happen. In happened to them in their time. It can happen to you!

"Therefore, since we are surrounded by such a great cloud of witnesses, let us throw off everything that hinders and the sin that so easily entangles, and let us run with perseverance the race marked out for us. Let us fix our eyes on Jesus, the author and perfecter of our faith, who for the joy set before him endured the cross, scorning its shame, and sat down at the right hand of the throne of God" (Hebrews 12:1–2). In the center of your cheering section, waving nail-scarred hands with a smile across His weathered face, stands Jesus, shouting encouragement. He will continue training you, every step of life's marathon, continually making you a living example of holy transformation. Now it's time for spiritual training.

NOTES

Chapter 3: Three Reasons We Fail to Morph

1. A. W. Tozer, *The Knowledge of the Holy: The Attributes of God, Their Meaning in the Christian Life* (San Francisco: Harper & Row, 1961); J. I. Packer, *Knowing God* (Downers Grove, Ill.: InterVarsity, 1973).

2. J. P. Moreland, *Love God with All Your Mind: The Role of Reason in the Life of the Soul,* Dallas Willard, gen. ed. (Colorado Springs: NavPress, 1997).

Chapter 7: Let's Get Practical! Or, God's Game Plan

1. William Barclay, *The Daily Study Bible Series, The Letters to the Galatians and Ephesians,* rev. ed. (Philadelphia: Westminster, 1976), 149.

Chapter 11: Why Trying Hard to Be Holy Doesn't Work

1. Dallas Willard, *The Spirit of the Disciplines: Understanding How God Changes Lives* (San Francisco: Harper & Row, 1988).

2. John Ortberg, *The Life You've Always Wanted: Spiritual Disciplines for Ordinary People* (Grand Rapids: Zondervan, 1997).

Chapter 12: God's Spiritual Training Program

1. Oswald Chambers, *My Utmost for His Highest* (Westwood, New Jersey: Barbour and Co. Inc., 1963), 195.

LIVING ON THE EDGE
with Chip Ingram

Chip Ingram is the teaching pastor and founder of the rapidly growing, nationally syndicated radio ministry, *Living on the Edge*. Chip can be heard daily on over 500 radio outlets nationwide, internationally in the United Kingdom, and worldwide around the clock via the Internet. Chip also serves as president and CEO for *Walk Thru the Bible* ministries, an international ministry committed to Bible teaching and application.

A graduate of Dallas Theological Seminary, Chip has a passion to communicate biblical truth through relevant, accurate teaching in a way that challenges listeners to put into practice what they believe in order to impact their world and beyond with the life-changing Gospel of Jesus Christ.

At *Living on the Edge,* it is Chip's vision to be used by God as a catalyst in

Transforming how America thinks about God,
How Pastors think about preaching,
How Churches think about their communities, and
How everyday believers live out their faith at home and at work.

Each week over a half a million people from around the world tune in to **Living on the Edge** via radio and the Internet to hear biblical truth applied to critical, everyday matters. Whether he is teaching through a book of the Bible, dealing practically with essential doctrines, or discussing hot topics, Chip's style of opening God's Word brings clarity and insight that leads to transformation in the lives of those who listen.

Those who hear **Living on the Edge** write regularly to share stories about how Chip's practical exposition of biblical truth has encouraged, challenged, convicted and illuminated their hearts, often with dramatic stories of total life transformation as a result.

Transforming how America thinks about God . . .
and how individual believers live out
their faith at home and at work.

You can learn more about the ministry of **Living on the Edge** by visiting our web site at www.LOTE.org or calling toll free at 888-333-6003.

Insightful Reading from Chip Ingram & Moody Publishers

Holy Ambition-
What it takes to make a difference for God

ISBN: 0-8024-5645-6, Cloth

What God is seeking, what He is looking for are not the brightest and the best. God is looking for people who are willing to live on the edge. People who so long to see God's agenda fulfilled in this fallen world that they attempt what seems impossible, ridiculous and "outside the box" for God's glory.

With piercing honesty and 'in-your-face' conviction, Chip Ingram challenges believers to make a difference for God. Using the Old Testament model of Nehemiah he offers hope to dislocated hearts, broken spirits and all of us. I highly recommend this book for the development of a Holy Ambition!

- Dr. Joseph Stowell, President, Moody Bible Institute

After all the shallow books on leadership, we finally have a biblical, balanced model in Chip Ingram's fascinating study of Nehemiah.

- Rick Warren, Pastor, Saddleback Community Church, author, *The Purpose Driven Church*

MOODY
PUBLISHERS

THE NAME YOU CAN TRUST®

1-800-678-6928 www.MoodyPublishers.com

SINCE 1894, Moody Publishers has been dedicated to equip and motivate people to advance the cause of Christ by publishing evangelical Christian literature and other media for all ages, around the world. Because we are a ministry of the Moody Bible Institute of Chicago, a portion of the proceeds from the sale of this book go to train the next generation of Christian leaders.

If we may serve you in any way in your spiritual journey toward understanding Christ and the Christian life, please contact us at www.moodypublishers.com.

"All Scripture is God-breathed and is useful for teaching, rebuking, correcting and training in righteousness, so that the man of God may be thoroughly equipped for every good work."
—*2 TIMOTHY 3:16, 17*

MOODY
PUBLISHERS

THE NAME YOU CAN TRUST

HOLY TRANSFORMATION TEAM

ACQUIRING EDITOR:
Greg Thornton

COPY EDITOR:
Anne Scherich

BACK COVER COPY:
Julie-Allyson Ieron, Joy Media

COVER DESIGN:
Becky Kimball

INTERIOR DESIGN:
Ragont Design

PRINTING AND BINDING:
Quebecor World Martinsburg

The typeface for the text of this book is
Berkeley